Beautiful Disasters

A Look Inside of Bipolar Disorder

(rerelease)

Also by Brooke Price

Beautiful Disasters

A Look Inside of Bipolar Disorder

(rerelease)

Brooke Price

Cover Art by: Michael Tolleson

This Book is dedicated to the beautiful disasters that allowed me to use their stories. You ladies are amazing. I am forever in your debt.

Contents

Acknowledgements

~Mr. Michael Tolleson: Thank you so much for allowing me to use your painting, "Shadow Walking", for this book's cover. It means the world to me and I believe it makes the book perfect. You, sir, are an amazing talent and I am lucky to have been given the chance to know you.

~Christina: You opening up and telling me the turmoil and darkness in your life is priceless to me. Your story touched my heart, even the things I left out of the book. I felt that something's are best left away from the worlds eyes. Thank you again.

~Heather: Babe you already know. We are so much alike. There is nothing that really needs to be said. There is something I want to say though. I wish I could've been there for you and your mother more than I was when we were growing up. I am sorry for that. Thank you for always being here for me despite me not always being there for you. I try though. Love you sis.

~Kay: Everybody knows it comes more naturally to us to fight. I'm glad, however, that we are giving "playing nice" some effort now. Still never thought I'd be thanking you in the acknowledgements of one of my books; however, I am with a smile. Thank you for opening and sharing with me.

~Andrea: You're a sense of solace to me. I've told you this before, thank you for that. Even when you are amid a break you'll try to listen to me. Anytime I have asked for you to help me with a book idea or chapter or title, you're there. This means everything to me and I only wish I had more I could offer to help you. Thank you so much for opening and allowing me to expose your most vulnerable parts to the world.

~Jennifer: I love you woman, you know this. Thank you for opening and sharing part of your story. I know it wasn't easy and I want you to know I appreciate it deeply. You mean the world to me, always have. Thank you.

~Leá: Thank you for being part of this book.

~Shelena: I love you sis. Thank you for giving me permission to write out part of your story. It's appreciated that you were willing to share a small chunk of your life. Without you I don't know what I'd do. Every day you make me a little bit prouder.

~Ann: Being able to include you in this meant more to me than I can express in words. You are still a young one but you are also very wise. Your candidness was much appreciated. You are special girly; don't you ever forget that. I love you baby girl.

Beautiful Disasters:

A Look Inside of Bipolar Disorder

(rerelease)

Picture Courtesy of Bing Images

"Crazy isn't a condition it's a place and it exists somewhere between Love and Oblivion"

—Stanley Victor Paskavich

Ch. 1.

The Facts

Bipolar Disorder is such a sullied term. It's defined as "a brain disorder marked by bouts of extreme and impairing changes in mood, energy, thinking, and behavior. Symptoms may emerge either suddenly or gradually during childhood, adolescence, or adulthood." (Nimh.nih.gov) All those nominal, evocative words are nice; however, I stand here to verify that Bipolar Disorder is enough to make you sick and to give you the ability to fly. It can reduce you to your bathroom floor with a razor blade or to being sleepless for days.

It changes how you behave, then it messes with you further by making you unable to care about your actions as you commit them. Bipolar Disorder spends your money in mania fueled shopping sprees, only to leave you unable to recall where the money went or what you spent it on. It isn't just in their heads or something they need to get over, nor is it an excuse.

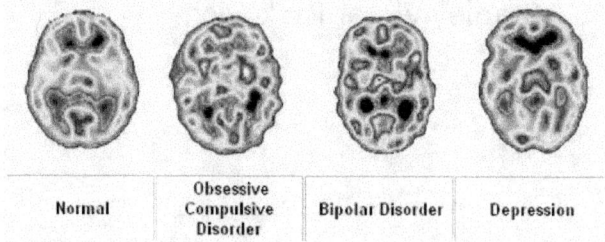

Picture Courtesy of Bing Images

Living with this disorder isn't a joke, as it is treated by some. More times than I can count I have heard men call their girlfriends "Bipolar" because she was happy one minute and mad the next. Your inability to keep your girlfriend happy isn't always indicative of her having Bipolar Disorder. People are way too quick to use having Bipolar Disorder as a way of explaining someone that is simply in a bad mood. Bipolar Disorder is so much more than a moody person. It is a mental illness that impacts every instance of a person's life.

Most people living with Bipolar Disorder can't control their emotions, i.e. why people use it as a joke. Even with serious help, sometimes they can't. I mean, no control; their irritation easily turns into violence and/or screaming at others. A moment of sadness can extend into 3 weeks of barely eating, over sleeping, or just lying in bed. People with Bipolar Disorder are plagued, almost followed, by their disorder. Does this still sound like it's just a mad girl to you?

Bipolar Disorder not only leaves its mark on your relationships and behaviors, it leaves its mark on your brain as well. Being simply moody most certainly doesn't do that to a person. In fact, researchers have been trying to make a diagnostic tool out of brain scans of Bipolar individuals for years. That is a literal statement. Bipolar Disorder causes measurable differences within the individual's brain.

Changes in the Brain of a Bipolar Person:

-Loss of brain tissue

-Memory loss

-Loss of facial recognition

-Co-ordination loss

-Disruption in Noradrenaline and Serotonin

-Reduction in the number of neurons

-Reduction in the number of glial cells

-Imbalance between Cholinergic and Catecholaminergic activity

-Increased concentrations of the stimulatory G-protein

(Institute)

To further prove this point I direct you to a study from Science Direct. In this study, they took "24 Bipolar, 20 Schizophrenic, and 18 normal comparison subjects." They then evaluated said patients using an MRI. Scans of the patients "temporal lobe structures including the amygdala, hippocampus, parahippocampus, and total temporal lobe" were assessed to "obtain volumes for each structure in the three subject groups." The severity of each patient's symptoms in all groups were assessed. The findings for the Bipolar group were interesting. They found that the "amygdala volumes were significantly larger in the Bipolar group than in both Schizophrenic and normal comparison subjects." The implications of this study are staggering. They are suggesting that there are significant differences in "affected limbic structures in patients with Schizophrenia and Bipolar Disorder." They go on to suggest that "these specific neuroanatomic abnormalities may shed light on the underlying pathophysiology and presentation of the two disorders." (Lori L Altshulera, 2000)

This disorder also affects the personal and business lives of those affected by it.

Having Bipolar Disorder physically affects your:

-Jobs

-Relationships

-Police records

-Family

-A person's credit

-Causes them to have psychotic thoughts

-Bad risks

-Act differently

-Reduces their ability to handle their stressors

-Can cause sleep disorders

-Causes bouts of not being able to recall spans of time

Individuals with Bipolar Disorder face hurdles every day, as do all people. With this disorder the hurdles seem to knock the wind out of you though. It is almost as if the hurdles are too high to ever get over. It's easier for some to just give up. One of the biggest hurdles was listed above. The inability to hold a job is almost universal. Scientist now estimate that the problem with jobs is, in fact, an outrageously big problem. They report that a person with Bipolar Disorder is a full 40% less likely to have a job then someone without the disorder. (McGrath) The kicker is that it affects more individuals than given credit for.

The statistics say that "Bipolar Disorder affects approximately 5.7 million adult Americans, or about 2.6% of the U.S. population age 18 and older every year." (Nimh.nih.gov). It isn't isolated to the borders of this nation either, it affects people of all nations. The statistics are incredible.

International Bipolar Disorder Statistics:

-Australia reportedly has about 238,957 people with Bipolar Disorder

-England reportedly has 723,248 people with the disorder

-Germany around 989,095 people with Bipolar Disorder

-Canada reportedly has around 390,094 people with it

-Iran reportedly has 810,038 people with Bipolar Disorder

-India and China each have about 12-15 million people with Bipolar Disorder.

 (Nimh.nih.gov)

While these statistics are alarming, it may give comfort to some to know that Bipolar individuals are not alone in their battle. This disorder can certainly leave a person feeling all alone. While no one is completely sure what causes Bipolar Disorder most believe it's an array of different things. A few are "proven" and a few are just theories.

Possible Causes of Bipolar Disorder:

There aren't many things that Bipolar Disorder can be contributed to. Things like these are our best guesses as to how it is developed:

"-**Biological differences**: People with Bipolar Disorder appear to have physical changes in their brains. The significance of these changes is still uncertain but may eventually help pinpoint causes.

-**Neurotransmitters**: An imbalance in naturally occurring brain chemicals called neurotransmitters seems to play a significant role in Bipolar Disorder and other mood disorders.

-**Inherited traits**: Bipolar Disorder is more common in people who have a first-degree relative, such as a sibling or parent, with the condition. Researchers are trying to find genes that may be involved in causing Bipolar Disorder. Much like most other mental disorders, no two people are going to present with the same symptoms, and few will be able to tie their disorder back to the same cause."

(Diseases and Conditions: Bipolar Disorder, n.d.)

To some, including me, it's scary that Bipolar Disorder can be inherited. In fact, somewhere near 2/3's of people with Bipolar Disorder also have a parent or a relative with Bipolar, or likewise, such as Unipolar Major Depression. (Bipolar-lives.com) I, personally, had no idea Bipolar Disorder was essentially inherited and partially related to how you grew up, until I was diagnosed with it. I thought I was worthless and everything was my fault (no matter what happened or what anyone said). It's been like that ever since I can remember. I've criticized myself, in my head over everything all day long, from an early age. I thought how I felt was because of something that I had done wrong and couldn't remember. Finding out the statistics gave me a sense of peace. It helped me figure out it wasn't just me, it was my genes. It allowed me to blame my genetics for part of why I have this candy covered curse. I just wish I'd been diagnosed earlier in life.

Since that day, I've learned the genetics behind Bipolar Disorder are intriguing. A simple google search will teach you these general points about the genetics of Bipolar Disorder:

-When only one parent is affected the child has a 15-30% chance of being Bipolar.

-When both parents are Bipolar that risk raises to 50-75%.

-If a brother or a sister have the disorder than there is a 15-25% chance the other sibling will develop it.

-If an identical twin has the disorder than there is an 85% chance the other twin will develop it.

(webmd.com)

Of the above, genetics seem to play the largest role. There are more in depth studies that can be found to prove the genetics of Bipolar Disorder if you look hard enough. A study from The Journal of Medical Genetics teaches the risk an individual faces of developing Bipolar Disorder more exactly. Per this study, "the approximate lifetime risk of Bipolar Disorder in relatives of a Bipolar proband are:

-Monozygotic co-twin 40-70%

-First degree relative 5-10%

-Unrelated person 0.5-1.5%.

Occasional families may exist in which a single gene plays the major role in determining susceptibility, but the majority of Bipolar Disorder involves the interaction of multiple genes (epistasis) or more complex genetic mechanisms (such as dynamic mutation or imprinting)." (Genetics of bipolar disorder, n.d.).

This same study suggests that the chromosomes that are of interest to researchers are:

-4p16

-12q23-q24

-16p13

-21q22

-Xq24-q26

They go on to mention that "chromosome 18 is also of interest but the findings are confusing with up to three possible regions implicated." (Genetics of bipolar disorder, n.d.) In my family, mental disorders are wide spread. Just among my siblings it is extremely prevalent. I have a brother with Unipolar Major Depression and PTSD; 2 sisters with Bipolar 2, BPD, Anxiety, PTSD, and Social anxiety; a sister with Bipolar 1, PTSD, Sleep Disturbances, BPD, Social Anxiety, Anger; a sister with just Bipolar Disorder; a sister with BPD and Social Anxiety; -I'm diagnosed Bipolar 2, Social Anxiety, Body Dysmorphic Disorder, Obsessive Compulsive Disorder, and Borderline Personality Disorder ; and I have a few other family members that would rather not allow everyone to know their diagnosis.

Whenever a person has duel diagnoses the 2nd axis diagnoses are called "comorbid disorders." Therapist's know that comorbid disorders are especially important when diagnosing and treating Bipolar Disorder. When you look at the available case studies you can see how important comorbid disorders are. A study out of Psychiatric Services online states that the "assessment of Bipolar Disorder must include careful attention to comorbid disorders and predictors of compliance." (Donald M. Hilty, 1999)

Comorbid Disorders are significant for more than one reason. Recent studies suggest that a Bipolar person's comorbid conditions can contribute to a premature death. We all know that individuals with Bipolar Disorder have an increased chance of dying of unnatural causes: such as suicide, homicide, and accidents. A study out of the Psychiatry Journal suggests that "over the past decade, there is increasing evidence that people with Bipolar Disorder may actually be at a higher risk of premature death from general medical disorders." Said study goes further into this topic, breaking down the various reasons that a Bipolar person may have a premature death. Per this study, "the majority of excess deaths among persons with Bipolar Disorder are secondary to comorbid general medical conditions. The causes of this excess mortality may include unhealthy diet, obesity, binge eating, sedentary lifestyle, smoking, social deprivation, living alone or being homeless or single, poor access to and less effective use of health services, biased attitudes among health care providers, failure of psychiatric providers to ask about or address medical problems, the "competing needs theory" (that is, health care providers might give precedence to conditions that need immediate attention while management of other conditions is delayed or forgotten), and comorbid substance use disorders. (Babak Roshanaei-Moghaddam, 2015)

Comorbid Disorders are not the only important subject when treating Bipolar Disorder. Awareness is just as important to our wellbeing. I have found it to be a common occurrence that people with mental disorders do not talk to their families much about their disorders. I didn't used to talk to family about it either. *I just **KNEW*** they wouldn't understand. It was hard enough to get everyone to understand my son and how his brain worked with his severe Autism. I decided not to bother with it for a long time. I was wrong.

It is very important to talk to your loved one about how you feel and why you react the way you do. Even if they don't understand it is still important to talk about it. It mustn't remain the big pink elephant in the room. It is important to raise the awareness for all mental disorders; Bipolar Disorder is no exception to this rule. The less people know about what is going on with you, the less they understand-leading to the possibility of more tension and judgements.

When speaking to family and friends about Bipolar Disorder it is essential to make sure you point out the different ways it can present in patients. What I mean is that Bipolar Disorder comes in two main "stages"-the manic and the depressive, and 5 main types. Mentioning and educating about both sides of it and the different types is important. Involving your family in your treatment will benefit your long-term Bipolar management. This can even be seen in research.

Per a study published on American Psychological Associations website, "Recently hospitalized Bipolar, manic patients were randomly assigned to a 9-month, manual-based, family-focused psychoeducational therapy or to an individually focused patient treatment. All patients received concurrent treatment with mood-stabilizing medications. Structured follow-up assessments were conducted at 3-month intervals for a 1-year period of active treatment and a 1-year period of posttreatment follow-up. Compared with patients in individual therapy, those in family-focused treatment were less likely to be re-hospitalized during the 2-year study period. Patients in family treatment also experienced fewer mood disorder relapses over the 2 years, although they did not differ from patients in individual treatment in their likelihood of a first relapse. Results suggest that family psychoeducational treatment is a useful adjunct to pharmacotherapy in decreasing the risk of relapse and hospitalization frequently associated with Bipolar Disorder." (Rea, et al., 2003) it MAY be HArd for You to believe...but living with this Sickness is fAr more difficult tHAN the PAiN it brings to You from MY Hurtful words. for You— You cAN escApe. You cAN WAlk AWAY from me At ANY moment. i AM left Here iN MY MiND. iN the PAiN ANd confusion tHAt is MY life.

Ch. 2

The Spectrum of Bipolar Disorder: The Myths and the Facts

Don't be confused, not all Bipolar individuals have such severe episodes of mania and depression. No disorder presents the same to any two individuals. Bipolar Disorder is **NO** different. As I stated previously, there are several different types of Bipolar Disorder. Five to be exact.

They are as follows:

1. **Bipolar 1:** *distinguished by its inclusion of a full blown manic episode at some time in their life, also typically severe swaying moods*

2. **Bipolar 2***: milder than Bipolar 1, these people go back and forth between depression and elevated moods, but never mania*

3. **Cyclothymic Bipolar Disorder***: like Bipolar 2, but less severe*

4. **Mixed Bipolar Disorder or Bipolar Not Otherwise Specified***: having highs and lows that coexist or jump back and forth quickly*

5. **Rapid cycling Bipolar Disorder:** *having several periods of depression and/or mania in a single year* (webmd.com)

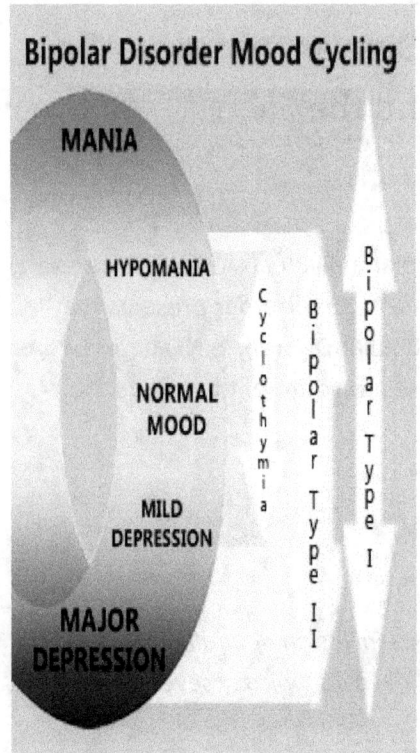

Picture Courtesy of en.eikipedia.org

Bipolar 1 can also be referred to as "Cade's Disease or Manic Depression." Originally it was referred to as these. Therapist used to lean towards using antidepressants to treat Bipolar Disorder. This trend has changed as of late. Now scientists are calling for less use of said medications. (S Nassir Ghaemi, 2002) Often Lithium is the first line of defense for doctors. This medication holds a higher rate of long term success than most. Lithium also has well documented anti-suicidal effects. As my previous therapist told me as he was prescribing it to me,

"Don't try to kill yourself with this medication, it won't work out the way you hope." The second choice of most professionals to treat Bipolar Disorder are usually prophylactic treatments like carbamazepine and valproate, although evidence of their effectiveness is weaker. (Prof Bruno Müller-Oerlinghausen, 2002)

Individuals with Bipolar Disorder are at a higher risk of many things; one of those things being the increased risk of developing Alzheimer's as they age. The general populations risk of developing said disorder is about 7%, an individual with Bipolar Disorder's risk jumps up to near 19%. This is a huge jump in numbers. Researchers have found a silver lining to this situation. They found a few years ago that not only does Lithium help with the treatment of Bipolar Disorder by helping stabilize our moods, but- it also helps reduce our risk of developing Alzheimer's as we age. The medication brings the risk back down to near the same level as the general population. (Paula V. Nunes, 2007)

Other things we are at risk for can be directly related to the episodes of mania and depression that we feel with our Bipolar Disorder. I realize that people who don't deal with this every day may not know what Bipolar Mania or Bipolar Depression looks like. Despite medications and therapy, it is possible that an individual will still have episodes. That makes it exceptionally important to be able to identify what type of episode said person is dealing with. I had no idea what the difference in the two were until I was diagnosed.

Symptoms of Bipolar Mania Might Include:

-Reckless behavior/poor judgment like being hypersexual or promiscuous or being a dare devil

-Being excessively distracted

-Racing speech and thoughts

-Talking more than usual

-Irritability or hostility

-Grandiosity, or an inflated sense of importance

-Elevated moods such as being extremely happy and it be inappropriate

-Hallucinations and psychosis

   (Bipolar-lives.com)

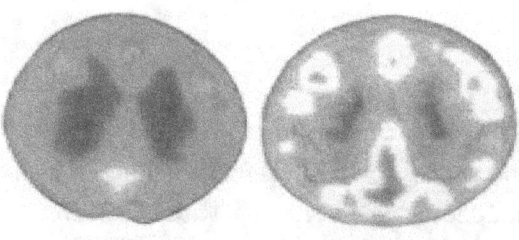

**Brain in
normal periods**   **Brain in
manic phase**

Pictures Courtesy of Bing Images

Symptoms of Bipolar Depression Might Include:

-Withdrawal from favorite activities

-Persistent feelings of sadness and crying spells

-Lack of pleasure in life

-Sleeping too much or unable to sleep

-Thoughts of death or suicide

-Fatigue or no energy

-Drop in grades or inability to concentrate

-Significant weight loss, weight gain, or change in appetite
(Bipolar-lives.com)

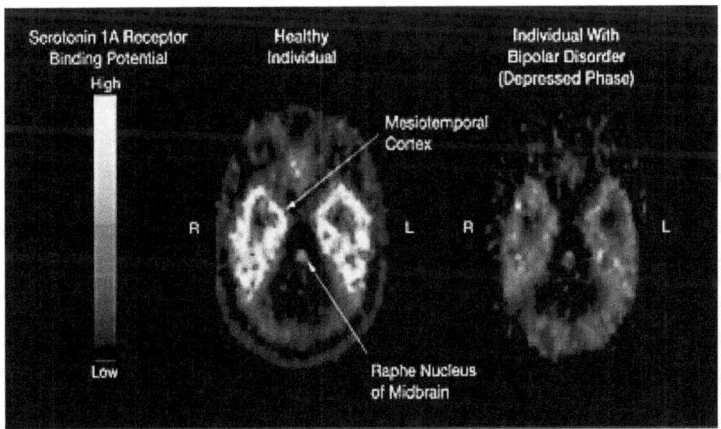

Picture Courtesy of Bing Images

Everybody experiences their mania and depression differently.
No two manic or depressive episodes are exactly alike, even in
the same individual. They can be like each other but rarely

follow an exact pattern of behavior.

Depressive episodes present with the following for me:

When I am depressed there are days that I do not want to move. Too many days. It isn't like when you have zero motivation and just don't want to get up. It's more than mental, my damn legs refuse to work. My head feels like it will explode into a puddle of tears if I lift it up more than an inch from my pillow. Often my shoulders feel like they have had spikes beat down into them. The worst part for me is that I in turn eat my feelings. I will consume more food in a day than any person should; just as counterproductive to my wellbeing, I reprimand myself the whole time I am doing it.

Plus, if I do manage to get up there is no way my brain going to work properly. I'm too focused on the depression, on something that was said to me or something that invaded my thoughts and won't leave. Too focused on faults in myself or on how worthless and pitiful I am, how ugly I am. I just cry and hide and try to forget me. I often think my husband used these times to his advantage with me. I may be wrong but it feels as though whenever we get into an argument he uses the words and phrases that he knows triggers me to send me into a depression. In my opinion he does this just to shut me up and end the argument swiftly. I have heard many Bipolar women claim this same thing of their relationships over the years.

When I get depressed I just want to escape reality, if you want the truth. Going into a depression doesn't happen easily in my life. I am more prone to episodes of mania than I am of depression Normally if I go into a depression it is directly related to something that my husband has said to me. He has known me so long that he knows the exact things to say to me to send me over the edge. I control myself a lot better now. When I was younger though he could send me into a week-long funk with any well thought out and placed sentence.

Through therapy I've learned a lot of useful coping skills to control this feeling. Used to the only option was to give in and cut to feel that release. That all so important release. The punishment for being sad in the first place. Some thing that makes perfect sense while doing it, yet makes no sense afterwards! I would spend days after I did it thinking about how flipping insane I must be. Who must bleed to feel, to hurt to be calm? I owe my therapist, Nancy, so many thanks for the skills she taught me to overcome these feelings of depression. I also owe her a thank you for helping me release some of my resentment towards the man I married for his role in my past episodes of self-harm.

The coping skills I learned were imperative to my healing. The truth is that sometimes my depression would become so severe I'd have a mental break with reality. I'd have to disconnect, lose control. I've found that those times are about the most dangerous time to deal with a Bipolar person. Those days rarely happen to me now. Like I said, I owe that progress to Nancy Martin and to the medication she helped me realize I should feel no shame for needing.

When Mania Hits, the Bipolar Manic Episodes present like this for me:

Some people's mania is submerged in thoughts of suicide. My mania isn't so much intertwined in suicide ideology anymore, used to it was. Now my biggest problem in mania is an inability to sleep, rapid speech, poor monetary choices, and having a high level of energy. I also tend to be more susceptible to anger when I am manic. Saying the wrong thing to me during a manic episode it could go many ways. It is very possible I could get violent. The scariest thing is that I can be perfectly fine one moment and the next be losing it, head all spinning around with pea soup coming out of my mouth.

With my high-energy level during mania comes insomnia. Days of insomnia that aren't helped by the fact that my Autistic son rarely sleeps either. My eyes feel as though they are glued open whenever mania hits. Normally about a day in I start to notice that I am in fact manic. Yes, I can tell when I am having a manic episode. A lot of individuals with Bipolar Disorder can, the distinction comes with years of studying yourself and learning your triggers. In addition to the insomnia I speak a mile a minute. My rapid speech during mania is not something that I notice happening as I am doing it, instead I am alerted to the fact that it is happening by the people around me. I am told to repeat what I said "but slower" all the time, by multiple people. Some days being told that irritates the piss out of me.

I have diagnosed OCD and one of my "things" is cleaning, no matter how cliché that may be. I also have a lot of other OCD behaviors but that is not where I am going with this. When I am manic I reclean everything multiple times and rearrange everything. I mean everything! Nothing is safe, and just because I have already moved it once doesn't mean I won't decide I want it somewhere else and precede to move it again. Not only do I clean but I organize and line everything up, I also have a tendency to cut my hair off and then become enraged that I was allowed to do so while in a manic fit. When I am in the grips of mania I also tend to come up with these grandiose ideas and attempt to follow through with them at all costs. I also make plans that I have no intention of keeping.

Making plans that I don't intend to keep isn't the only social sabotage I commit whenever I am manic. I also tend to demonize my friends and family members. I will pick one or two out at random, subconsciously of course, and just pick them apart. Sometimes I do it to their faces and sometimes I do it to myself. For the duration of my manic spell I will be angry with said people. There have been times that I have become angry with somebody that is very important to me and the reasoning behind my anger never happened. Generally, when that happens it is over a perceived feeling I got from them. I also do this whenever I have an episode of "splitting" as related to my Borderline Personality Disorder; however, whenever I am splitting it is more than just a bad attitude towards the person- I hate the individual for an extended period and immediately set forth removing them from my life. When I'm manic I do not block the person on social media and erase their phone number, etc. That is the sort of thing I do whenever I split. (This is an example of how BPD and Bipolar Disorder can mirror each other)

Another issue I sometimes experienced whenever I am manic, pre-medication, is that I also had the tendency to experience hallucinations. Whether this is more due to my Bipolar Disorder or my BPD is up for debate. Personally, I believe it is a little of both. Many individuals with Bipolar Disorder also claim to have experienced hallucinations, whether visual or auditory. What I do know for sure is that they used to drive me nuts.

Living with Hallucinations:

When some people think of a hallucination they think of the 1960s and 1970s when everybody was taking L.S.D. That is not the type of hallucination I am talking about. There are different types of hallucinations. Not everybody that hallucinates sees visual hallucinations. Some, like myself, have auditory hallucinations. As with most things in life, everybody that has them experiences them different than others. They can be severe, where you are leaning towards a deeper diagnosis; some can be somewhat mild, where they annoy but are manageable. A great deal of people I have interviewed that hallucinate have auditory ones. It'll sound like someone is constantly behind or next to you whispering your name continuously or making random noises repeatedly.

In addition to living with the highs and lows of this disorder there are a few things that are generally almost always seen in someone with Bipolar Disorder. For one, Bipolar individuals tend to self-medicate. They drink and/or use illegal drugs or prescription pills to cope with the feelings of being "crazy," of being unstable, of feeling so empty. That's not the only typical thing you see with Bipolar individuals though.

Typical behaviors or traits seen in Bipolar individuals:

-Impulsive acts, as I said before. (Therapists even use this fact to gauge a client's likelihood of committing an impulsive violent act. However only about 50% of Bipolar individuals have issues with violence.)

-Some sort of trauma in their early life. Something that impacted them down to their core. A situation/event that hides in their dreams every night.

-Substance abuse problems

-Abuse in their childhood

-Legal Troubles

(McGrath)

Since you now know all the basic facts about Bipolar Disorder you should also be aware of the myths floating around. Even I'm guilty of believing some of these. When people do not know enough about something they tend to assume. Assuming something can slow progress for people that are suffering from it.

Myths that I've heard:

- **"Treatment is a cop-out"**,

This comment dumbfounds me.

- **"You just need to think positive"**.

Let me remind those people that Bipolar Disorder is a treatable mental disorder. It affects the person's brain. Telling someone with this disorder to 'think positive' is like asking a diabetic to control their blood sugar with their own will power or looking at a solider with PTSD and telling them to man up. *It doesn't work that way.*

-**You shouldn't have kids if you're Bipolar.**

Well, I didn't know I was until I was almost 30. I was misdiagnosed several times. Most of us are. My biggest problem with this one is the unspoken stigma/myth there. Insinuating I **shouldn't** be a mother. Bipolar individuals are as good a parent as any person without Bipolar Disorder. They also possess the ability to spot anything going on with their kids that may indicate a mood or personality disorder.

- **'There is NO suicide issue, few people actually try it'.**

I would like to point out that in our country suicide is high ranking on the leading causes of deaths. About 25,000-30,000 people take their own lives each year and about 85-90% are said to have a mental illness, such as Bipolar Disorder.

(Nimh.nih.gov)

-Medications are habit forming. That they change the people's personality, no one recognizes them and that a person can't be counted as sober if they are on the meds.

If our medications are taken as prescribed they are not habit forming. Most of the time they prescribe us Lithium in the end. Most of us start off on other meds and our doctors changed our meds many times before they gave us lithium. As for changing our personalities. Not really, but they do level us out. I think of it as being like meeting the real person for the first time. When you have spent your life trying to cope with the feeling of being a spilt person, it's hard to figure out who the hell you are on your own let alone show yourself to another person. I suppose you can only grasp that if you personally lived/live with it.

Knowing the difference between the facts and the myths doesn't really give you a complete idea of what it's like to be Bipolar. You must escape reality and immerse yourself in stories from suffers. Soak up all the knowledge you can about what it is and develop the ability to understand not everyone thinks like you- nor do they feel like you, handle stress like you, or have grown up like you. That is, if you want to understand this disorder.

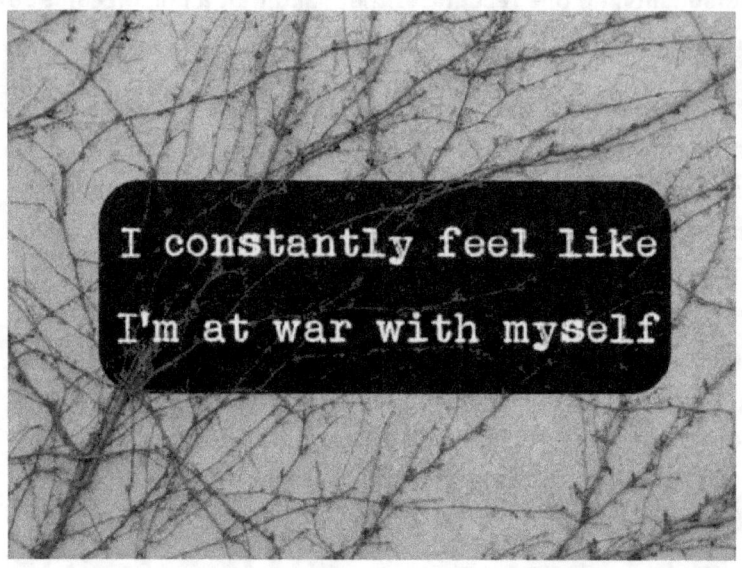

Picture Courtesy of Goggle Images

Ch 3

The Bipolar Disorder/Borderline Personality Disorder Parallel

I briefly touched base on comorbid disorders in the previous chapters but there is one comorbid disorder to Bipolar that warrants being singled out. Borderline Personality Disorder is a disorder that presents with symptoms that often mirror those symptoms of Bipolar Disorder. The mirror is such a close one that it has recently come to light that many people that are diagnosed with Bipolar Disorder may have BPD instead; or, in some cases Bipolar Disorder is a comorbid disorder to BPD.

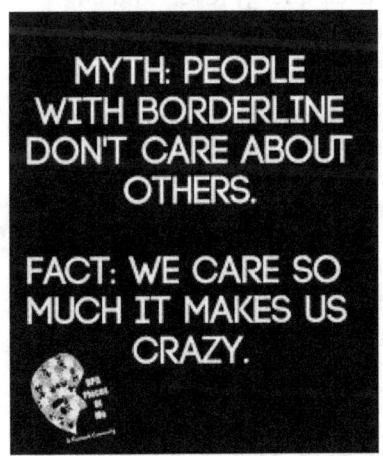

Picture Courtesy of Pinterest.com

The comorbidity of BPD and Bipolar is believed to be high by many psychologists. The research I have done is mixed, it appears that some believe that Borderline Personality Disorder is comorbid to Bipolar in around 12% of cases and some believe that it is more like in 40% of cases. (Tracey M. N., 2013) Either way, I am one of the people that hold a duel diagnosis. The combination of the two disorders makes it very hard to cope with my emotional responses every day.

The confusion comes in when you start looking at the symptoms of the two. Anger is a huge issue for people with both disorders. Both Bipolar Disorder and BPD leave the sufferer with bouts of irrational anger. The key difference is held in how the anger is presented. In Bipolar Disorder anger is more closely associated with the shifts in mood from depressive states to manic states. There are also reports of hypomania in Bipolar individuals where a person may be easily angered. Hypomania is more commonly characterized by increased energy levels and an unwavering dismissal of sleep though. In people with Borderline Personality Disorder their baseline mood tends to be anger. It isn't so much a matter of shifting from mania to depression as it is just an everyday thing.

Another key difference in the anger shown by people with these disorders is that people diagnosed with BPD frequently experience shifts in their moods from moment to moment. The shifts happening from one mood to another in a matter of minutes. Their mood shifts also seem to rely heavily on the actions of others in their lives, whereas the mood shifts of a person with Bipolar Disorder are more unpredictable. Often these shifts come out of the blue. According to Psychology

Today, "all personality disorder issues manifest in relation to interpersonal relationships." (Federman, 2014) In other words, personality disorder (BPD) symptoms are triggered by conflict within relationships and mood disorder (Bipolar Disorder) symptoms are not.

People with BPD also do something called "splitting" whereas people with Bipolar Disorder do not. Splitting is the "black and white thinking" that people with BPD engage in. The textbook definition is, "a term that describes difficulty with the ability to hold opposing thoughts, feelings, or beliefs about oneself or others." (Kristalyn Salters-Pedneault, 2016) People with BPD are unable to join the positive and negatives of everyday situations and people together into a unified pattern of thoughts when splitting.

According to (Kristalyn Salters-Pedneault, 2016), "splitting is both a distorted way of thinking and a coping mechanism used to keep yourself from feeling hurt or rejected". This can include the all or nothing thought process or the belief that someone is all good or all bad. Glorifying a persons every move or demonizing it over the smallest thing. Another symptom that is mirrored in both disorders is impulsive behavior. Being impulsive is an extreme issue dealt with by people with both diagnosis. When a person holds a duel diagnosis of Bipolar and BPD it becomes an even bigger issue.

Individuals from both diagnostic groups will tend to have issues with impulsivity. Whether it be them being impulsive in actions or in words. People with BPD also lean towards being very impulsive in their love lives, regularly. Their impulsivity also seems more long-term. Individuals with Bipolar Disorder have breaks in the impulsivity and their other symptoms. Individuals with BPD do not have long breaks in their symptoms.

A recent study by Mark Zimmerman, M.D., from the Department of Psychiatry at Rhode Island Hospital and the Department of Psychiatry and Human Behavior at Brown Medical School on the two disorders points out more differences. (Pedersen, n.d.) involved "interviewing 268 participants between 1995 and 2012. Of these, 62 participants were diagnosed with Bipolar II depression and 206 participants were diagnosed with major depressive disorder with co-occurring Borderline Personality Disorder."

The study found several key differences between BPD and Bipolar Disorder. To quote said study, "The findings reveal that patients with Borderline Personality Disorder are more likely to have additional disorders and also more likely to have experienced childhood trauma than those with Bipolar Disorder. They may also experience longer and more severe episodes of depression... Depressive episodes are a considered a part of Bipolar Disorder, but depression is a separate disorder that can co-occur with Borderline Personality Disorder ..." (Pedersen, n.d.)

When looking at the relationships of both diagnostic groups and found that individuals with BPD are "less likely to be married." When comorbid disorders where looked at the study showed that, "38 percent of the BPD group were diagnosed with three or more non-personality disorders (anxiety, mood and eating disorders) compared to 26 percent of the Bipolar group. Thirty percent of the BPD group were also diagnosed with post-traumatic stress disorder compared to 10 percent of the Bipolar group." (Pedersen, n.d.)

A significant difference the study found that is also worth mentioning is that the "BPD group also had longer depressive episodes, were more depressed overall, had a harder time doing day-to-day activities, and had significantly more childhood trauma events — especially physical neglect — than the Bipolar group. This group was also more suicidal, with twice as many BPD participants as Bipolar participants reporting three or more suicide attempts." (Pedersen, n.d.) The only factor the study found to be more common in individuals with Bipolar Disorder was that genetics seemed to play a larger role in Bipolar than in BPD.

The oddest
things hurt me.
They get stuck
in my head
and replay over
and over.

MPLYRIEZ.COM

Picture Courtesy of Pinterest.com

~Step into the Home of Insanity~

~True Stories from Women

with Bipolar Mind's~

Everyone sees who
I appear to be,
but only a few
know the real me.
You can only see
what I choose to show,
there's so much
behind this smile...
you don't even know.

Picture Courtesy of Bing Images

Ch. 4

The Unbreakable Woman:

Christina's Story

(Ohio)

Christina and her husband

Christina is one of the sweetest women I've ever had the privilege of meeting. She probably has one of the heaviest stress loads imaginable. She has chin length brown hair and an infectious smile. When she listens to someone speak she genuinely listens, a rare quality in a person. Christina's issues with Bipolar Disorder started before the age of 17, which is typical for onset. She describes it as being as if she woke up one day and suddenly felt like she'd lost her mind. She describes herself as an extremely hyper teenager, hyper to the point of there not really being words to describe it.

During our interview, she told me that she started to act incredibly impetuous; her thoughts about other people were starting to slip away. It was becoming as though there was never going to be any consequences to her actions. Thus, she pushed the limits as much as possible, as many Bipolar teenagers do. One day she stole her mother's credit card and went on a shopping spree. Not one time did Christina stop to think about what her spending was going to do to her mother. How she would feel; if she'd be mad?

Or maybe, just maybe, she thought about those things the whole time and just really didn't give a damn. Truthfully, it's a toss-up as to which. Shortly after the incident she started having issues with insomnia (again like most of us). She'd be up for days at a time. It felt like she never needed to sleep, like she could take on the world. In these moments, it feels almost as though your eyes become robotic. You can know that you are tired but it doesn't matter, your eyes WILL NOT allow you to go to sleep. We are talking 48-72 hours awake or more.

A lot of us experience times of promiscuity too. Per normal, Christina did as well. Likelihood is she just wanted to feel complete, to feel normal on the inside. Promiscuity can be used as a method to self-medicate, minus the illegal drugs. These actions drove her to start cutting. It's very confusing after you cut, especially the first time. It's almost like an incapability to cope with what you did to yourself and at the same time feeling so much better because you did it. I can't imagine how hard this must've been for her as a teenager.

Luckily Christina had a fantastically supportive mother who took her to get help. A lot of times Bipolar individuals are left untreated until around age 25. Christina was auspicious in the fact that she didn't have to wait that long. Her doctor prescribed her Depakote and Ativan. After a while she started to feel better, to feel normal. In fact, she felt so normal that she thought she was cured. This is a typical feeling among us. We feel relief for the first time and think the medicine fixed us. She was somewhat stable and wasn't cutting so she made a mistake and went off her meds. This is also very common in people with Bipolar Disorder. I believe that so many of us do this in a desperate attempt to take back control of our lives. Most of us HATE taking medicines every day.

Christina and her mother

Because she didn't have the meds to help stabilize her, she starting cutting again. The release of her anxiety by the blade was like one of the best drugs around, as she even said to me while I was interviewing her. Problem was, by this point she was cutting all over her body. This included her face. It got so bad, she reports, that one time she needed stitches in her forehead from a self-inflicted wound. This incident put her into the psych ward, which again put her on meds. She says that going back on her meds after taking herself off caused her to have a great sense of guilt. She felt ashamed.

This did however help her realize she needs her meds. She'd had a small break from the cutting, but as she said, "the urge to cut would win in the end, and with a huge victory too." Soon after, she spent all her money-leaving her feeling lost, insignificant. Like most Bipolar individuals, she couldn't account for what she'd bought with her money, the time was blank. Again, with much luck, her mother helped her with her essentials. Christina felt a massive sense of guilt from this as well. She began to feel like her meds weren't working, so what's the point? Again, she went off them.

This time her impulsiveness manifested itself in a different way. She began to self-medicate, she started drinking. Christina told me one story where she woke up in a Walmart parking lot, in the back of her car, unaware of how she got there. She felt so scared and so alone-so helpless, so confused. She was trying to numb herself with alcohol. Her anxiety and her mania were certain to drive her insane. Soon after she went back to the hospital to figure out different medication combos.

She indicated to me that it was hard to admit to having Bipolar Disorder to others. She'd hear supportive comments like, "It's no different than being diabetic, you can't control it," but all she could think was, "How do they know? Society hears the word Bipolar and treats you like you have the plague."

Eventually Christina got married and her husband became her rock. He is so accepting and supportive, he certainly helps her stay on track. As Christina said, "He showed me love when everyone else looked at me differently because they didn't understand." Christina was given a whole new reason to stay on track after her marriage. John and Christina became parents to a beautiful little boy. Her son is not only an Autistic angel, he is also Bipolar.

Christina and her son, Chris

His diagnosis was traumatic for Christina. She felt a deep sense of guilt knowing she passed the gene on to her son. Knowing what his struggle is going to be like. It was almost too much I'm sure. Through that fear and pain, she found strength to figure out how to raise her angel. She learned that she can help her baby through his manic stages and help him understand it. She always tells him that he's unique and that different is beautiful.

Bipolar Disorder has dulled her long-term memory, as it has many- including myself. It leaves us with vague recollections of past events. We can mostly thank the medication we so desperately need for that. However, despite her lack of detailed memories she wanted to share a few experiences to help some others hopefully understand.

Despite being Bipolar I've noticed Christina is an extremely zealous individual. She is extraordinarily devoted to her family and staying on track. She currently takes Lithium and Lamictal to handle her mania. Both medications caused her to have bad stomach cramps at first, but the pain is always worth the gain. Christina tells me that she has mellowed out quite a bit as she's aged, which gives me hope. By age 32 she had leveled out more with her manic phases. She attributes this to her husband, John, and his inexhaustible support for her, and to taking her medicine every single day at the same time.

She told me that once she got herself dedicated to her health and taking her medicine properly she had something happen she never thought would. Her mother told her the she was so proud of her. I understand the need, the desire to hear those words. A person can be supportive of you to the end of the stars but never once express that they're proud of you. When you hear this from them it's such a strong feeling you can barely process it. I can't figure out how to express how much it touches me to know that she got that from her mother.

Unfortunately, in 2008 Christina's life changed forever- putting all her progress with her disorder at risk. Out of nowhere her mother unexpectedly collapsed on the floor. They would soon learn that she had suffered a brain aneurism. The doctors couldn't do anything. They placed her on life support, 100% brain dead. The next day her family made the excruciating decision to remove her from life support. The strength Christina must've needed to get through this is inconceivable, but she did and she keeps going every day to honor her mother's memory.

Everyone could take a lesson from that.

I can tell you one thing for sure, my life will never be the same since meeting her. I'll never understand how she's able to find the strength to deal with her own mind, let alone her son's mind. I live with Autism too (my oldest son is diagnosed), I know what she goes through. Our life is hard, I'd say it rivals living with many other disorders.

This woman is to be admired.

YOU CANNOT DESTROY ME.

I DESTROY ME.

Picture Courtesy of Bing Images

Ch. 5

A Complete Source of Amazement:

Heather's Story

(Indiana)

Heather

Heather is only 21 and has been through enough grief to make a normal person lose their mind. She has the most beautiful eyes, that look deep into your soul and she has the softest hair. She can be your best friend or your worst enemy, depending on what you say to her. She is just as soft as she is hard. Getting to the soft side is a challenge though.

She grew up before her time and never got a chance to find who she is. I watched Heather grow up. I've watched this girl struggle and cry as she learned how harsh this world is. I watched her grow from this little girl into a beautiful soul, and then into a stunning mother. I love this beautiful disaster because she gets me and because she is always there. I love her because she is my little sister. Not only that, as she grew she became one of my best friends.

Growing up Heather had an absent father. He was beyond absent, he was blissfully random. He was loving, when he wanted to be. The rest of the time he beat women, lied and refused to show up for his obligations. I remember her being so enamored with him, he was her daddy. She thought he hung the moon. I also remember her slowly drifting away from him as she matured and picked up on what he was.

When Heather was 6 her father used her to get my mother to come home from the battered woman's shelter she was staying at. When my mother unlocked the door, all hell broke loose. Two pieces of my heart where stuck in that brutality for hours. At that young age, she watched her father unmercifully beat my mother for over 10 hours while hiding under a table, terrified. He trashed the house beating her. In the end my mother was unrecognizable and Heather was changed forever. She may not realize it, but I watched her change after that. I believe this was one of the most influential occurrences on her Bipolar Disorder coming out.

Heather's mother, on the other hand, is the kindest woman I've ever met. She would give you the shirt off her back if you needed it. She's always been there for all of us. She, however, raised 2 children on her own-their fathers didn't help. She struggled, in fact she did without so her kids could have every day. These times of struggle caused the family to be homeless on numerous occasions.

Heather and her mother

Heather's mom always made sure there was somewhere to go and food to eat. It's just hard for kids to understand how much parents struggle, especially single parents. Those factors combined left Heather with a lot of childhood trauma. By 13 she started cutting to release it.

When she was in 7th grade she was given shit about her cutting scars by a boy in her math class. He saw her scars, which she always wore a hoodie (even if it was 90 degrees outside) to cover. Instead of acting like a normal human being, he acted like a teenage jerk. He revealed Heathers arm was slashed up to all their peers sitting around them. He was loudly telling them she was "emo" and that "she cut." Heather was so infuriated and so confused, (and I'm sure she felt violated) that she acted out of anger and impulse. She stabbed him in the thigh. She then broke the pencil off in his leg.

However, I do believe the most traumatic event for Heather, unsurpassed to this day, was the death of a guy she was incredibly close to. Despite the things that her father put her through being unimaginable, this day defined her. There are a few times in every life that something happens that completely changes who you are, how you understand the world. I believe this was one of those instances for my sister. This guy was her heart. You could say he was like her other half.

The back story is that he'd just had surgery on his knee right before this incident. Heather was helping him at his house.

Since his surgery, they had him on a lot of pain killers. This particular day he had passed out after taking some. From here Heather has a hard time recounting the events of that day. She did her very best whenever I interviewed her though. Talking about this invokes so many emotions still.

After some time, her friend woke up screaming. It was immediately clear that he wanted her to leave. She was confused by this sudden reaction but also didn't want to upset him. Doing the only thing she knew to do she started up the stairs. That's when she heard it. Her friend was grabbing for his gun. As he slid the gun off the table Heather made a beeline for his bed, determined to intervene in whatever plans he had. In a split second, she was at his side, trying to grab the gun. She did all she could think of to stop him. As it was happening he grabbed and pulled her away from him by her hoodie. At the same time, he pulled the trigger. His hair and blood splattered all over Heather. She blacked out.

The next thing she remembers, as she tells me, is waking up in the hospital while being admitted right alongside her friend. The whole situation left a lasting mark on Heather's life. The events after his death added to her anguish. To put it in her own words, "To top it off, even though his autopsy indicated that it was a suicide and I couldn't have done it, the police still interrogated and investigated me for his death."

When Heather started to come back to reality after this

happened she really couldn't cope. She lost herself. She didn't know how to function normally because it felt like her brain wasn't working. It wasn't just a self-contained feeling, we could all see her cracking. She explained it as a feeling of not knowing who to be. She secluded herself from everyone while trying to figure out how to cope, as you would suspect, she blamed herself. Even though a regular person would see how irrational feeling guilty because you are unable to stop a suicide is, for minds like ours- rational isn't always our strong suit. We place blame on ourselves for everything.

Not long after this Heather tried to hang herself. It was devastating to everyone that knew of it happening. She also ate a ton of Clonidine and ended up in the hospital in a separate attempt on her life. It frightened the crap out of us. Since his death, Heather has had over 50 stitches in her arm. To this day, I wonder if she cuts because of the guilt, or because of the pain of not being able to understand. Maybe it's because she's trying to figure out why she has had all these obstacles and sorrows to overcome, or maybe it's a combination of these all.

Like many of us, in a few short years Heather has tried several different medications. Most of them have not helped at all, even at high doses. She has also been admitted, inpatient, at the psychiatric hospital on 3 separate occasions. It's a matter of persevering and never giving up in your quest for a healthy life. Heather still perseveres and I am so proud of her for it.

Heather has tried these medications:

-*Celexa*

-*Seroquel*

-*Prozac*

-*Effexor*

-*Trileptal*

-*Zoloft*

-*Ambien*

-*Abilify*

-*Sonata*

-*Elavil*

-*Xanax*

-*Vyvanse*

-Depakote

-Remeron

-Paxil

-Geodon

-Clonidine

-Buspar

-Cymbalta

-Trazodone

-Sonata

-Divalproex

-Oxcarbazepine

Currently she is taking Depakote alongside a few other meds. They seem to help her quite a bit, if she keeps on a medication routine. Taking your medications at the same time every day is imperative to any person with a mental illness to reach success. Along with everything else she also has issues with insomnia. These incidents of sleeplessness are not concurrent with manic episodes. There are weeks that she can't sleep and weeks that all she wants to do is sleep. In addition, she also has anger issues-much like a large percentage of us. Her anger and rage can stretch beyond the normal Bipolar reaction however.

Heather's anger almost always takes her to a bad place. She tries her hardest to remain on a calm level but when pushed she explodes into a force to be reckoned with. In the past few years, Heather has been arrested on 3 separate occasions for resisting arrest and so forth; because she flies into a rage and loses herself. The people around her call the police for her protection and the protection of themselves and it sends her even further into a rage. She has a hard time accurately recalling the moments before and after the arrests. She has been informed that the first time it took 6 police officers to restrain her, the second time it took 2 and excessive force was used on her because of the first incident. To me, this seems more like a BPD

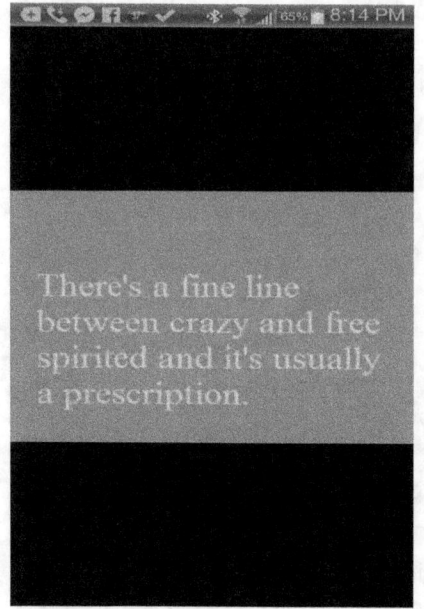

There's a fine line between crazy and free spirited and it's usually a prescription.

Picture Courtesy of Google Images

trait than a Bipolar trait.

These incidents of rage were present throughout Heather's life. When she was younger, after the death of her close friend, her shrink wrote her a prescription for Prozac. Her initial reaction was to rip up the prescription and throw it in her face. To Heather Prozac was a waste of time. Being her initial reaction, of course, that is exactly what she did. She also made sure the lady realized that she was in fact a "troll fucking bitch." Want another example of Heather's anger issues? When she was in junior high a classmate slept with her ex-boyfriend. Her reaction was to kick the girl's locker into her face while she was getting her books out. She split the students face open.

Now, at 21, motherhood has calmed her down quite a bit, but not completely. It's changed her enough though. She is an amazing mother as well as an amazing human being. Her sons' and her daughter have given her reasons to live. Mental illness is going to be a struggle her whole life; however, if anyone can withstand the battle, it's Heather.

She recently married a man named Billy. He is her world. Her rock. They have their issues, as all marriages do. He is trying to help and understand what is going on in her head with everything he has. They have had one little boy and one little girl, in addition to her oldest son. They have a great family life for the 3 children and a great love for each other.

Heather and her family

Heather is a source of admiration for me, as the title of this chapter suggests. I can't think of too many people in this world that can deal with what she has thus far and still come out of it breathing. I wish that I held half of the strength she does inside of myself. Maybe if I did I'd make it through OK. She reminds me that I can do the things I don't think I can. That anyone with Bipolar Disorder can find a tiny bit of happiness in every day, especially if their happiness is as cute as my nephews' and my niece.

When she
transformed into a
butterfly, the
caterpillars spoke
not of her beauty,
but of her
weirdness. They
wanted her to
change back into
what she always
had been.

But she had wings.

        — Dean Jackson

Picture Courtesy of Goggle Images

Ch. 6

What being raised by a Psycho Can Do:

Kay's Story

(Indiana)

I've known this woman for a long time. We've had a very sorted past with one another but refuse to let that define our relationship. Both of us being Bipolar has been a challenge for us. Not to mention we mostly hated each other for most our lives. To an outsider our friendship must look fake or insane, but we get it.

Kay's a tiny little thing, always has been. Her personality is anything but petite though. Our relationship is an odd one. I think we both have a realistically mutual fear of seeing what the other is capable of. The basis of us knowing each other has always been hatred and astonishment; a lot of which was fueled by men. It was a vicious decade long roundabout of fighting, at the end of which we decided being friends is the best solution. I guess we look at the situation as us preserving mankind by saving everyone from our war.

Kay had a very traumatic life, one that was near unbearable. Her mom is pretty much pure evil. She was a drug addict when Kay was small and is a drug addict now. Constantly in and out of prison. That woman treated her kids like an afterthought, it was heartbreaking. Everyone figured out by age 4 or 5 that there was a problem with Kay. Whenever her mother would "act out" on her, as she put it, she would beat her arms against the floor violently. In doing so she broke several fingers. That's how hard she would beat them. She recounted how once while at her aunts she was informed she had to go back to her mother's- her answer to this was to run her head into the wall until she passed out.

By kindergarten and 1st grade Kay was already getting kicked out of school due to her anger. When she reached junior high the school finally tried to take steps to help, as lax as the help was. They decided a brother/sister situation would be the magic answer. More than help her it seemed to annoy her. It certainly seemed to frighten the brother/sister worker. The sister accidentally broke an item Kay had bought at the mall, causing Kay to completely lose her cool. Shortly after, her anger was shifted towards her teachers. It got so severe that they ended up suing her parents. Kay had to go to court because of it.

The court decided she needed therapy and anger management; she was to do both until she reached 18. It didn't take long and she'd thrown a chair at her therapist, which broke a window. This lack of impulse control and anger sent Kay to the hospital in the back of a police car. A thing that struck me as interesting (as well as true to myself) is that Kay remarked that the court's decision pissed her off because at the time she couldn't identify what she was doing wrong.

They have tried many medications on her:

-*Celexa*

-*Lexapro*

-*Luvox*

-*Paxil*

-*Prozac*

-*Welbutrin*

By age 13 she had started drinking to numb herself. About the same time her mother had gotten her little brother addicted to drugs. He had overdosed several times; because of her mother's actions Kay's little brother spent much of his early adulthood in and out of prison, much like his mother had. Her mother's drug use also worsened as Kay aged.

From there Kay's drinking increased. She started smoking pot and taking pills when she could get them. They bounced from place to place- hotels, their car, RV's, rat infested homes, etc. The fear of sleeping in these homes helped her withstand when she can't sleep now. By now her mother's issues had spiraled out of control. She'd been ripping off drug dealers and the 3 of them had to go on the run. Eventually she attempted suicide. Her life had finally turned her into a person that wanted to hurt everyone and everything just to show them her inner turmoil.

When Kay hit her teen years' full force she ended up in one bad relationship after another. Not because of her behavior so much as her attraction to the bad boys. One that sticks out the most to me was her relationship with my ex-best friend. This dude was messed up and made the trust issues she had worse. He cheated all the time and lied about his drug use. He also stole from her. I'd have to say he was more damaging to her than anyone else ever had been, except maybe her mother.

She's been separating herself from the people that trigger her lately. It's helped her a lot. She still has major anger issues, like most of us with Bipolar Disorder do; she also has lost memories as well. She is really trying though. Kay has had a life no one should have to live. Her mother is a thorn in her side that pops up occasionally, throwing all the memories back into her face.

It's going to take an eternity to recover from everything, but I must say she is making a good attempt. I wish her all the luck in the world with it. She just made the biggest transition in life that a woman can make- she became a mother for the first time! This is something, I must say, that none of us ever considered a possibility for her. I hear passion in her words now, that's something that hasn't been present for a long time. Her daughter and her fiancé have changed her life for the better. They have shown her what family is.

I have never
ever been a blue
calm sea.
I have always
been a storm.

Ch. 7

Growing Up Without an Identity:

Brooke's Story

(Washington/Indiana)

Me

Until I was 8 I had an almost perfect life. What I can remember of it anyway. We lived in the country alongside a large chunk of my father's family. My father's father was sheriff of the county I grew up in. Had been for years. We had free run of the whole "town," we explored and ran all day long. As an adult I have few memories from my childhood that I can bring forward clearly. The ones I can suggest to me that it was the best time of my life. Not remembering it bothers me terribly sometimes.

A memory from where I grew up

When my parents divorced, my life fell apart, as it does for most children. That's when I found out that the secure reality I had, my bubble, was all a façade, a fake. My parent's love for me certainly wasn't fake, just the situation surrounding my existence. I am extremely guarded about this part of my life. You see, I found out that my dad had adopted me.

I know my parents could've never anticipated how hard it was going to be on me to find out, who could've? They were trying to protect me; my father would never purposely hurt me for anything on this earth. He's always been my daddy and he always will be. I love him with everything I have. Unfortunately, their intensions really didn't matter because despite their efforts the truth damaged me deeply. Portions of it are still visible today. We don't talk much about it, in fact- we don't talk about it at all. It is a silent and tense subject in my family. What makes it even harder is the other people involved in the "lie."

The other people involved happened to be little girls. The fact is that I had sisters, and no one ever told me until then. Within the same year that I found out that they existed I was introduced to two of them at our local carnival. It wasn't a beautiful situation like that sentence might suggest. It was damaging. We lived in a small town, everybody was at that carnival- the whole town. It felt like the town was watching the high school scandal of the early 80s finally play out in front of them. The biggest thing I was obsessing over was the fact that I knew that my father was somewhere at the carnival and possibly watching this introduction.

As I grew I realized that a great deal of people probably knew my entire life what was going on surrounding my birth and nobody said anything to me. That night at the carnival was like the town secret finally coming out. Brooke meeting him with her mother and his wife standing nearby. (My mother and 2 of my sisters' mother were best friends in high school-and still are to this day.) I remember thinking about how uncomfortable it was meeting them and their dad while my dad was wondering around the same carnival. The whole thing is a lot to throw at a kid of my age.

As I grew more the sense of everything being my fault, the sense of how ugly I was began to take me over. I had a great deal of depression following me; however, I could never pin point what exactly was causing it. That added to the problem. I noticed that everything that was said to me upset me. It wasn't until later in life that I realized I really had a problem with any form of self-criticism. It crushed me. I took it so personally. That is more my BPD than my Bipolar Disorder though.

My mother has always been a beautiful woman. She has the sweetest heart, but she hasn't always had the easiest time. I remember watching her wear shoes with holes in them and thrift shop shirts (the same ones for many years in a roll) so that we would have what we needed. Of course, my father helped her. He never let us go without the essentials, if he knew we needed them. He paid his child support and clothing allowance every time he was supposed to and he spent time with us. It still didn't make the split and life afterwards easier on her. She started out as the best mother on earth. Then after the divorce things got rocky for all of us and they are just now starting to calm for my mother, all these years later.

In my youth, we moved a lot, a whole lot. I recently spoke to my mother's 2nd husband. A man that means the world to me. We spoke about how often we moved as I was growing. They (him and my mother) hated how much they moved us, they felt great guilt over it. I never knew that. As I grew she about lost her mind a few times. She always had rage issues as my little brother and I grew. He was a very difficult child to raise. I have never seen anything like it. On top of trying to care for 2 children after the divorce she was also divorced a few times. I do believe that she took it harder each time.

Towards the time of my high school graduation, she was in an abusive relationship that changed her forever. I spoke about this man in Heather's chapter. To sum it up, I'd say that she had a great start as a mother, a rocky middle, and has finished it off landing just where she needs to be.

However, that part of my life is not for public display nor did I write this book to remind my mother of her past. With that said: She has become the best mother and the best Mimi on earth. What road she traveled to get to that point does not matter. All that matters is who she has become because of the road she took. She's supremely supportive of me and my family, she loves us fiercely.

Moving on.

Into my teenage years, I found a group of friends that could show me how to make all the bad thoughts go away. Their methods weren't the finest but they worked for me at the time. I was about to dive deep into the world of drug abuse. Deeper than I ever care to admit or discuss. After the first party I was hooked. Some would even say I was out of control. I started shop lifting and getting in trouble with the law. I was promiscuous. I partied all the time, my drug usage increased and I started using stronger drugs. I have memories of stopping on the side of the highway as a teen and dancing in the rain on the center line because I felt as though I should. I did this on multiple occasions. I also have memories of breaking onto the school's soccer field to run through the sprinklers at 3 am.

Around age 15 I got sick. I had E-coli in my kidneys that had started as a simple bladder infection. It had been ignored and let go for way too long. It was a time in my life that I felt very neglected. Not long after I was admitted my mother had to leave on the semi with her (then) husband. This is going to sound bad on her but she really had no choice. It is a real possibility that if she had refused he would've beat her to death. I just wish she had woken me up to tell me goodbye. When I did wake and realized she had gone in the middle of the night I felt a piece of me fade away. It broke me.

She was gone for nearly a year once she left. I moved in with her parents, I lived there for a long time. They are amazing people that mean everything to me; however, I felt like I was alone and my mind was constantly messing with me. Plus, they'd already raised their children and I felt it wasn't fair that they were now raising me too. It was then that my moods started swinging more than ever before. They were unpredictable at best. To top it off, I could never sleep. If I ate I spent an extended period vomiting it back up, not to mention I had no idea who I was inside of myself. I had no identity. My mom's marriage to the man was torture on us, her most of all. On her first return visit home, she showed up with a huge swollen black eye. We were told that he accidentally elbowed her while changing a tire.

This weighed heavy on my mind at the time. I wanted to believe what my mother was telling me though. Left to my own devices and allowed to make basically all my own decisions from the time my mom left on that semi-truck I started down a path of making every wrong decision I could make. I decided I was going to spend most of the week at my boyfriend's house once I hit 17. Not long after that I was learning about meth and becoming a borderline alcoholic. However, when it came to my drugs I didn't discriminate, I'd do just about whatever was put in front of me. I even listed my 23-year-old boyfriend as my emergency contact with my high school my senior year, that way he could call me in to school and nobody would ever know.

My, then, boyfriend and my little brother

I got out of hand very fast. In fact, one night I ate right under 15 Ambien with my friend because he said it'd be fun. I sure do wish I could remember if it was or not. I have no actual memories from that night after we agreed upon the number of pills we could take. We based this decision on the fact that it took 21 to stop his heart the last time he'd taken them. At that time our logic seemed sound. Maybe a month after the Ambien incident I was given 30 Adderall XR and decided the best option I had was to snort every single one of them within 10 hours with my cousin. I almost died, literally. I ended up not being my best option, a faux pas on my part. It took days to recover from that little mistake, didn't stop me from continuing to use though.

Me before my Senior Prom

You must remember that during that time I didn't see my dad much, or my mom; and my grandparents wouldn't have been able to tell you what a person on drugs looked like if their lives depended on it. I had little to no supervision, so I acted accordingly. I did so for several years. It didn't help that I also had issues with authority and functioning well in school. I got into several violent fights during high school. Truthfully though, I wasn't at school often-I skipped school more than I went.

Around the same time, I was about to graduate high school my auditory hallucinations started. Normally just whispering or shouting of my name but every occasionally, I'd hear horrible things about myself. To this day, they drive me insane, late at night especially. I do not have them all the time. Do not think that I am saying that. It is mostly brought on during times of stress.

Me, my senior year

In that same year, I got married to a man that had been a close friend of mine for several years. On the eve of our wedding we took pictures of me in my wedding dress snorting Adderall off an elegant mirror. The day of my wedding I spent most of the morning snorting them to calm my nerves. How I ever thought that'd work I don't know. I am not proud of this. I could've easily left it out of this book. I am leaving it in to show what mindset I was in when I made such an important life decision. I am leaving it in to show other people that our actions don't always make sense and that it should be a red flag for our loved ones. Ultimately, the point is: I was out of control. I had no children, no responsibilities, and I was about to enter into a legal contract of marriage with a man that had about as much of a sense of maturity as I did. The odds were against us.

There wasn't a single guest at our wedding that had full faith in the union they were witnessing. My mother even expressed afterwards that she only expected it to last 6 months.

First dance at our wedding

Well, not 6 months later we found out I was pregnant. While not all of it was expressed to me and never has been, I can only imagine the things that were said once the news got out. The snide comments about what kind of parent's we'd make and how we'd probably crumble under the pressure. I am sure that most people were scared that we wouldn't grow up and stop "partying." To everyone's surprise though, as soon as I found out I was pregnant my mind snapped and I quit everything cold turkey. I went from this out of control teen to a soon to be mother with the disposition of Betty Crocker. Oddly it happened within 5 seconds. It was like I changed into a different person overnight. In hindsight, the fact that I could switch that fast is terrifying and quite symptomatic.

Not long into the marriage my husband started getting to know the "other side" of me. At first, he was annoyed, you could see it in his eyes. He thought I was being a brat. It didn't take long for him to develop a sense of respect mixed with a sense of fear towards the different "sides" of me. At this point in my life I was still largely undiagnosed and completely unmediated. I struggled every single day. When our son was born, there were complications. He was put in the ICU for a long while. He was in a medically induced coma, having seizures. It traumatized me more than anything else in my life thus far has. I wrote about it in my book, "Living Through Autism's Eyes: My Journey with My Son."

I wrote the following of our son's birth:

"At 8:06 pm, November 19th, Zain Mikeal was born. I pictured his birth through my whole pregnancy. He'd arrive. Chaz would cut his cord. Zain would cry his first cry. We would all cry as well. I'd feed him for the first time. Pretty much standard. His birth was nothing like this, and little did I know then, his birth would scar me for years to come.

I pushed my precious child out, Chaz cut his cord, and then nothing, and still nothing. No cries, no handing my baby to me. It was silent. I remember looking over and Chaz was frantic, standing by the warming table. I was utterly confused as to why my sister, Shelena, had stopped filming. It felt like I was in a dream. I was out of it because of the epidural, so the gravity of this situation didn't hit me until later. Plus, nobody came right out and told me my son wasn't breathing. For the next 6 minutes, I'm sure it felt like the world stopped for my husband. I know if I had comprehended it fully I would've been losing it, so

I must give him serious props for holding it together for me.

Finally, at 8:12 pm we heard Zain cry for the first time. We were parents. He was 8 pounds 1 ounce and 22 inches of beautiful. He had blue eyes from the start and blond hair. Holding him put my heart at peace for the first time in my life. I felt complete. He was beautiful. I have been lucky enough to feel that feeling twice in my life, there is nothing like it. Zain seemed fine, we were all relieved. Until 2 days later.

On November 21, 2003 I was brought my son in the middle of the night to feed. I was alone and dreadfully scared, like first day of kindergarten or first day of a new job scared. Chaz had to go home that night to return to work, which I didn't oppose, but didn't like either. I tried and tried to get Zain to latch on as I attempted to feed him, but he wouldn't. I sat there and stared at him trying to figure out what to do and ultimately feeling like a failure. I noticed he was 'twitching' so hard that I thought maybe that is why he wouldn't latch on for anything. This wasn't really a 'twitch', but I have no other words to describe what my newborn was doing. I had never seen anything like this before, ever! I buzzed the nurse and she told me it was normal for newborns to twitch some. I tried to believe her, I tried to chalk up this 'twitching' to just normal newborn stuff like she said, but it didn't seem right. I had this feeling in the pit of my stomach. I couldn't just let it go. It didn't take me 10 minutes after buzzing them that I was buzzing back frantic. I didn't know what was going on, but I needed help. He wouldn't stop this 'twitching'. The nurse came, took one look at him laying between my legs, grabbed him and ran. She didn't even take his bassinet, just him, and ran!

The hospital I was in has their maternity ward set up in a circle. It makes it where new moms can see the nursery from their room window, across the court yard. It is all encased in glass. I remember watching the nurse run with my son in her arms, put him down on the table in the nursery and nurses surrounding him. I watched them work on Zain for what seemed like eternity. Finally, the nurses realized I could see them from across the way and closed the curtains. The closing of the curtains symbolized a lot to me. I know now I was reading more into it than I needed to, of course they were going to close the curtains, but I really obsessed over it in that moment.

The next 4 hours I spent waiting to find out what was going on. I found every single thing to obsess over that I could. The curtain, that damn curtain, was it symbolizing the end of my time as a mother? Would my baby make it? Was it like the end of a play? Why didn't she take his bassinet? They said they never take the babies or bring them without the bassinet, so why didn't she take his? Why has it taken 2 hours, 3 hours, 4 hours now to come tell me what is going on? Are they standing in there looking down on my son's dead body trying to figure out what they are going to tell the 19-year-old mother of this dead infant? My mind was going to bad places and I was still alone."

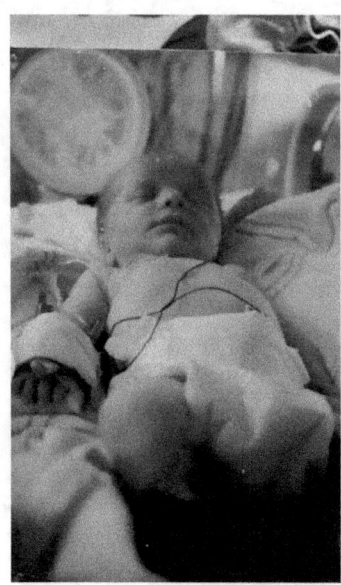

Zain in the NICU, in a coma

The trials in his life didn't end there. He was admitted to the
NICU following that and stayed there for almost a month, in a
coma most of that time. I refused to leave the hospital. As he
grew he acted odd, almost uncontrollable. It was impossible to
deal with when it was just him; however, when he was 3 we
added another child to the mix. I gave birth to my son, Dryden.

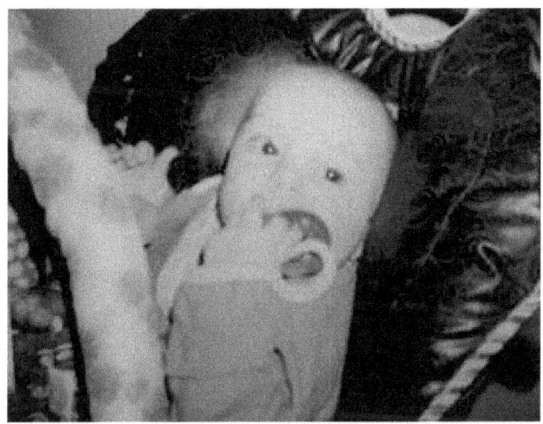

Dryden at 3 months' old

Around the age of 4 we found out Zain was severely Autistic. He didn't speak a word until he was 6 years old. The time spent trying to teach him was a battle. I spent many days and nights beating myself up during this time. I was so stressed out and rapid cycling quite often. Thankfully he's a little more capable of functioning now, which takes away a tad bit of the stress. His lack of words was a huge trigger for me, no matter what though. I just wanted to hear his voice.

During the time that I was trying to get Zain to talk for some reason my husband decided to cheat on me with a best friend of mine. Worse, he started doing this after we found out I had reproductive issues. I had several surgeries, including a full hysterectomy. I had to have harsh treatments, and the whole time he was running around. It broke me. I lost all ability to trust anyone in the amount of time it took him to make one life altering decision. I know this, I didn't want to live. I felt like I wasn't good enough and that if I were he wouldn't have done it. I fell into a depression, followed by a bad state of mania.

The hardest part is-he blamed me for years. As a result, I went into hyper gear. One minute I'd be depressed, the next I'd be ready to kill them both, then I'd just go numb. I felt like I was cycling way too often. I spent many nights alone in my room with a knife. Just crying and trying to make all the pain go away. Eventually my husband took the knife and hid it, to this day I can't find the thing. To be honest I sometimes I'm unsure how he survived those years but he did. The early years of my adulthood are textbook examples as to why therapy and medications are so important for mental illnesses. These things should be more easily obtained when needed.

Zain at 18 months

In the past years, I have tried many medications. Some I have wanted to try and was unable to because of the above-mentioned reasons.

I have tried:

-*Wellbutrin*

-*Buspar*

-*Xanax*

-*Prozac*

-*Lexapro*

-*Zoloft*

-*Abilify*

-*Klonipins*

-*Paxil*

-*Celexa*

-*Seroquel*

-Lithium

-Depakote

-Gabapentin

-Haldol

-Geodon

Starting on the meds was hard. Lithium was one of the first I tried. It hurt my stomach horribly. I laid awake many nights, not because of my Bipolar Disorder, but because of my treatment for it. I had tremors all night, violently. After a few weeks, it made me randomly vomit, violently; sometimes it was hours straight, most of the time in the middle of the night. The Lamictal hurt my stomach also. That only lasted about a month or two luckily.

Dryden at age 3

When on Lithium and several other medications you must have regular blood work done to monitor your levels and your internal organs. After one such checkup I found out that I'd overdosed, or went toxic, off my lithium. I was so sick and out of it for weeks until it was fixed. It was then that I found out the only way to treat extreme lithium toxicity is by giving the patient several rounds of dialysis. I am so lucky it wasn't to those extreme levels.

Zain and Dryden, ages 12 and 9

Despite the use of medication and therapy, I still have episodes. Though nowhere near as bad as I used to. I'll never be "cured," but I've learned that I can be more rational.

"Even so, I must
admire your
skill.
You are so
gracefully
insane."

Anne Sexton

Ch. 8

The Most Beautiful Disaster of Us All

Andrea's Story

(Indiana)

Andrea

Andrea is one of those people you can't forget once you meet. At first you think it's because of her appearance, then you realize it's because of her soul. I can't accurately describe her hair because if I tried it could very well be a different an hour later. Her eyes are deep and haunting and her mind is dark and commonly in turmoil. She hides her pain with tattoo's and piercings; she's a lost soul looking for herself in a sea of confusion. She's also caring, friendly, and loving- if you are deserving of it that is.

Andrea's problems with Bipolar Disorder started around the age of 16. She became depressed and was placed on Zoloft not long after she had her first child, a little boy. After having him her depression became serious. To be exact, it was postpartum depression. If you don't know what that is you should look it up. It is no joke, trust me. Being prone to postpartum depression and outbursts after giving birth makes complete sense. Studies suggest that hormonal influences appear to play an important role in Bipolar Disorder. It is well known that both the postpartum period and perimenopause are associated with increased incidence of mood disorders, suggesting that any woman that has just had a shift in hormone levels and is Bipolar may be at heightened risk of an episode. (Annemiek Dols1, 2011)

In 2007 Andrea had an episode where she "flipped," as we lovingly call our transition into the psychotic us. In usual Bipolar fashion, she can't recall what happened. She's told that she tried to kill someone. When checked into the hospital psych ward she failed her drug test for:

-*Cocaine*

-*Meth*

-*Weed*

-*Benzodiazepines*

Soon after that her year spiraled so out of control that she ended up in jail. At this point she was cognizant enough to recognize that she had a problem. This realization pushed her to ask for help. The decision to get help wasn't all that hard though, she'd just found out she was going to be a mother again. Nothing is more important to Andrea then her children, those kids are her whole soul. The help she received happened to be the doctor placing her on Klonipin through her pregnancy. Once her daughter was born she was switched to Seroquel.

Andrea and her children

Psych meds are hard to deal with, the constant increases and decreases we go through is mind numbing. Like any other person with a personality or mood disorder Andrea has been through several diagnoses. We are often misdiagnosed several times before we receive the correct answer.

-In 2008 Andrea was diagnosed with dysthymic disorder, anxiety and panic disorders, and Bipolar Disorder type 2.

-In 2010 her diagnoses changed. She had to get use to a whole new reality. Now she is told she has Bipolar Disorder type 1 and Generalized Personality Disorder.

-In 2013 it was changed again to Bipolar Disorder type 1, Borderline Personality Disorder, with anxiety and panic disorders

-In 2014 it changed again

A few years back the father of her children, who she isn't with anymore, was in a serious car accident. They had an incredibly toxic relationship. Without mentioning the things this man has done to make her break I will tell you a few things she has done to him.

-At 18 Andrea took a 12-gauge shotgun, safety off, fully loaded and tried to shoot him.

-She also has stabbed him in his eye

-On several occasions, she has knocked him out without feeling guilt.

Even after these examples she still cares about him. Hearing of his wreck scared her, it terrified her, and it brought out her dark side. Unfortunately, about the same time her (then) boyfriend left her. Upon seeing her children's father after the wreck coupled with the reality that she wasn't with her boyfriend anymore, she lost it. They placed Andrea in the psych ward for a week. While in the hospital she can remember them shooting her up with Thorazine and dragging her to her bed. To keep her stable, they put her on 1000mgs of Depakote and Clonazepam. While in there she was told that she tested positive for benzodiazepines and meth. Thing is, to this day Andrea can't remember doing any meth.

She has, like a lot of us, been a cutter for a large chunk of her life. That's a hard thing to learn to overcome. Therefore, I must give her credit for being able to control it the way she does. When she absolutely needs to cut, when she needs that release, she goes and gets another piercing or tattoo. I do that sometimes too, not as much as I should, but I do. It's no doubt why she's substituted one for the other, she doesn't want her children to ask her about the scars. She said this way her babies will "just see their mommy's pretty art."

Andrea has had a rough road to travel but she's still going. She wanted to give up on numerous occasions, but she's still here.

That shouts volumes to her strength. She's such a force, one to be reckoned with. Her story is one of perseverance. It is also a story of a mix of love and of hate. She's one of the best friends a person can ask for and one of the worst enemies you could make. I wish her clarity and comfort through the rest of her life. I hope to be able to call her my friend for years to come.

Image Courtesy of Bing Images

Ch. 9

Love, Music, and Insanity:

Jennifer's Story

(Arizona)

Jennifer

I met Jennifer almost a decade ago at our husbands' band practice. Little did we know then but during that first band practice we both made the deepest connection either of us had

ever dreamed of. She has the most exquisite hair that smells like honey and freedom; her eyes: they scream, "Hey baby, did you bring your knife?" To know her is to love her and to love her is to be auspicious.

Between the bonds formed because of the band, us being pregnant at the same time, and really having no other choice we became inseparable during that time in our lives. Her husband was the band's singer and mine was the drummer. Those were good times, musical times, times of love.

One of the earliest signs something wasn't right with Jennifer was at the age of 6. Jennifer lived on a military base; even then she hated her life. At some point, she was informed that her friend, someone she cared deeply about, was going to be moving. This news broke Jennifer's heart. Instead of crying like a normal 6-year-old she settled on revenge, and that revenge was best directed at the people moving into her friend's house. She snuck out and went over there (with her sister in toe) packing oven cleaner, watermelon seeds, and the intent to destroy. I'd love to be able to say that her sister came up with the idea and Jennifer was just an innocent accomplice- however I know her to well for that.

Once in the house they spit watermelon seeds everywhere and sprayed the house down with oven cleaner. It would've been the perfect crime had they realized the response time of military police. When the police showed up Jennifer and her sister proceeded to beg the police officers to take them to their grandmother because they didn't want to go home to their dad. They were told that the police hadn't seen two children so determined to not go back to their father, ever. Yet, they took them back and dropped them off.

From an early age Jennifer has had issues with self-esteem and with trust. She still does in her mid-30s. Looking in from the outside who could blame her. She has been abused, lied to, cheated on, drug through the mud, and her heart stolen from her in a court of law- three times. It's amazing this lady is still functioning. She may not be perfect, none of us are, but she surely hasn't deserved the things that she's been through.

Around age 13, while living in Washington, a game of hide and seek became a memory that has haunted her every time she's closed her eyes since. During that game, Jennifer was raped by a peer, someone she was supposed to be safe with. All the kids were playing; Jennifer thought she'd found the best spot, the one in the shed behind the tool benches. As she put it, "Guess I was right and wrong. I was there for 15 minutes and just as I thought they'd forgotten, here he came. He found me, pushed me up against the wall with his hand over my mouth, told me yelling would not be cool everyone was just having fun and this was part of it, pulled my pants down and then I was no longer a virgin."

Per Jennifer's account, she tried to tell her parents. The retort she got was not the one she expected. They told her she had just started her period that was all. In addition, her dad told her she was lying; he could report it but then she'd go to jail for lying. Not long after they moved from there to Arizona. Jennifer was agonizingly depressed over the rape, thus there wasn't much that mattered to her. You see the one thing she'd wanted to be special for her had been ripped away. It-made it where she couldn't see any reason to hope, to go on. Thus, Jennifer started to party hard.

She started doing things such as:

-Drugs

-Smoking

-Drinking

-Sleeping around

-Stealing Cars

-Damaging others property

Like many of us, Jennifer didn't care what she was doing or who she was hurting. At age 14 she came up pregnant. Her parents were less than thrilled and made an abrupt decision to tell Jennifer that if she didn't have an abortion she'd be sent away from her mother, that her mom would never be in her life again. She had the abortion and subsequently fell into a major depressive state, followed by extreme manic swings. She skipped school constantly and she'd have older guys over whenever she felt she wanted too; conveying no respect for her parents.

As a teenager, Jennifer had countless issues with boyfriends cheating on her. One instance involved a man of Mexican descent. At this time, she lived in Arizona with her parents, this man had become very special to her fast. When she went home she called to check on him and a woman answered the phone in the typical "Who the hell are you" fashion. Of course, this led to the typical argument over who is the man's actual girlfriend followed by feelings of anger, resentment, and embarrassment. Jennifer acted accordingly- she informed the other woman that the guy is her boyfriend and she was just wanting to tell him her AIDS test came back positive, he may want to be tested (Surely adding in there that the woman should get tested too). After the conversation, Jennifer walked away feeling justified and insanely happy over how the events had just conspired.

Around the age of 16 Jennifer met her oldest daughter's father. Shortly after she got pregnant she moved out of her parent's house and in with his parents. She lived there for some time before the abuse started. It was verbal at first, then it got worse. He started smacking her in her face and pulling her hair while telling her how worthless she was. At the same time,

Jennifer had to endure finding out that her boyfriend, the father of her child, was messing around with her sister.

After an altercation, based on that reality, Jennifer decided to move back in with her parents, pregnant. Her daughter's father went to jail; however, when he got out on parole Jennifer acted impulsively and moved him in with her and her parents. Within one month of moving in he was beating her again (while pregnant). While down the street from her house, her boyfriend came down there and started yelling at her- Jennifer warned him to go back to the house because of his house arrest but he wouldn't listen.

It was that day that Jennifer could feel the satisfaction of the revenge she so deserved. As she elegantly put it, "I proceeded to make him feel how he made me feel. I beat his ass, only hit him with the wood 4 or 5 times, but with the nails he couldn't move or breath. When his P.O. showed up I begged her to take him for good." This time he went to prison; however, he'd still call her mom. One day Jennifer received a letter from him, when she opened it all she could so was cry and cry. He had threatened to cut her unborn child out of her stomach if she wouldn't be with him. This chilled Jennifer to the bones.

Another example of how reckless she was when she was younger- while pregnant she drove a stolen car to her mother's house to confront someone that was there. Once Jennifer is mad there's no turning her off until she is ready to do so herself.

The whole drive there she must've been pumping herself up with thoughts of what it was going to feel like to be in that man's face, to see his fear, to smell his sweat. Not to mention the adrenalin that had to be coursing through her veins from driving a stolen car. Its things like this that feeds minds like ours, sometimes.

Once she arrived at her mom's house she ran in on the man, getting in his face and threatening his life with a butcher knife. After her verbal assault on said guy Jennifer went outside and slashed two of the man's tires with the knife. Several days later the same man drove by Jennifer's apartment and shot at her, everybody on the balcony dropped, accept Jennifer who stood up shouting, "Go get you lessons 'cause your fuckin aim sucks." Anytime anyone thinks about or speaks of that day they are still in reverence of Jennifer's lack of fear.

On the journey of life, I choose the psycho path.

Picture courtesy of Google Images

A couple of years back Jennifer's (ex) husband started smoking meth at an alarming regularity. He incessantly ran off for extended periods of time without feeling the need to inform his family where he was going or what he was doing. This led to dangerous spells of domestic violence and him cheating. I remember her sitting at my house on New Year's Eve waiting for her husband to come home, to kiss her at midnight only to have him never show.

I sat there listening to her tell her oldest that her "Daddy" was probably stuck in traffic or lost track of time, then listened to her finally break and say, "Baby doll, I don't know if he's coming back. It's ok though, we'll have a New Year's together." Once her daughter passed out I sat and watched her cry. It was heart breaking and showed the truth of who her (ex) husband was and the despondency she must've felt to get the hell out of there, but not knowing how too. We later found out he was with another woman that night. I don't speak to Jennifer or her ex-husband often anymore but I could still smack him for his behavior towards her that night.

Picture from that New Year's night, before her husband took off

A few years before that, at their daughter's birthday party, her (ex) husband was too busy with himself- with his band, drinking and hanging out, to start the food for his daughter's party. Two hours into the party he hadn't gotten up to do so, I ended up cooking the burgers for that party myself. The sad part is that anytime any of this was brought to his attention he made sure to make known that it was Jennifer's fault, not his own.

Not long after that, in the wake of a horrible fight, Jennifer packed up and left; this was the hardest, most devastating, yet somehow good choice of her life. She had no way to take her daughter with her when she left and she knew he'd never hurt her- so she left her there. A few months later she showed up in court to fight for her daughter only to have a bias judge set on his stand and pass judgment against her as he passed judgment on the case. She lost custody and was ordered to pay child support as well as being given bi-weekly visitation. Over time this had happened with all 3 of her children. Her parents mostly raised her oldest daughter, her middle daughter was raised by her father, and her youngest is being raised by her paternal grandparents as of now.

The trouble that Jennifer has had most of her life, outside of her behavioral issues concerning her Bipolar Disorder, have been both legal problems and problems within her family. A dynamic that has carried on from childhood. You see, all she's ever wanted to do is prove herself, be seen for herself, be loved as deeply as she loves, and to have her children. It seems at every turn she is blocked in the exertion, whether it be here own fault or the fault of others.

Jennifer's oldest daughter is 18 years old now. This girl is simply amazing (big surprise there, she takes after her momma). I fell in love with the girl years ago, when she was still a little girl that played with dolls. She has lived with Jennifer's parents most of her life, that didn't take away from their relationship though, they have a deep bond. She is in college now, I couldn't be prouder.

Her middle daughter is 15 years old; I have never had the pleasure of meeting her and somehow, I doubt I ever will. I have always imagined that she has either blue or hazel eyes and somewhat wavy brown hair, surely her mother's attitude. I don't dare ask if I am right though. Jennifer's middle daughter has been with her dad for several years, against Jennifer's will. Recently her father contacted Jennifer about their daughter, it crushed Jennifer and still does (she just doesn't talk about it). She is currently entangled in a legal battle over back child support for this child. It bothers her every single day, I am sure.

The youngest is 10, she grew in her momma's belly at the same time my youngest grew in mine. She is a special little girl. This kiddo has this adorable Shirley Temple hair and giant eyes that draw you in. Her sense of humor if right on, she is the kid that everybody wants but no one can have. As previously mentioned Jennifer lost custody of her and is currently locked in a custody battle with the paternal grandmother. This battle has been ongoing for 4 years now. She has visitation rights with this child.

Jennifer and her youngest daughter

There are many examples of her anger issues, her tendency to be promiscuous (in the past), and of her greatness and compassion in and for life. Her transitions between manic and depressive aren't as severe as mine but still bad. Without her medication, it's much harder to maintain control, she should be given serious props for her attempt to do so though.

Throughout the years, Jennifer has experimented with drugs to cope with her issues; self-medicating is often a measure taken by Bipolar individuals. For some time now she's been "homeless." Sure, she has places to stay but that isn't the same as having a place of your own. As far as I know, she has no insurance making it near unpractical to obtain her medicine, an unfortunate truth for thousands of Americans. A truth that no person should have to live with, no person should have to choose between money for their medicine and being sick. It isn't rational nor is it right. The situation that Jennifer has found herself in bothers me every day. Not out of pity but out of love.

Jennifer has beat the odds repeatedly in her life. She has problems just as bad, if not worse, than anybody else with a personality or mood disorder. I miss her every day and hope that she has found peace in her life. As I stated before, I had a deeper connection with her than I have ever had with just about anybody in my life.

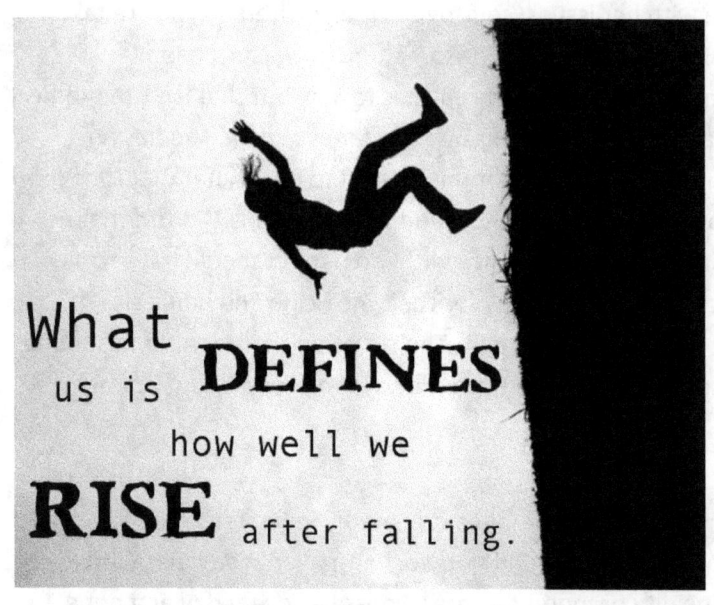

Picture Courtesy of Google Imaging

Ch. 10

Finding Strength while Searching for an Answer:

Leá's Story

(Tennessee)

Leá is my brother's ex-girlfriend. They have 2 children together. At the time that I did the interviews for this book she was still dating my brother. Despite trying to be nice she definitely was not my favorite person in the world. Since that initial interview a lot has changed. One thing hasn't changed though- she still isn't my favorite person.

With that said, she has long blonde hair (sometimes), and long brown hair others. When you speak to her the sweet "southern" tone in her voice makes you unsure if you want to hug her or make sweet tea with her. Once you get to know her most people realize that it's neither. The feeling that her voice provokes is often actually uncertainty. Leá is Bipolar, just as I am, and just as it is with all other individuals with Bipolar Disorder- we have vastly different stories. Hers is enormously different than the other women I have written about. I am going to tell it as accurately as I personally know; from what she told me during our interview for this book and from what I have witnessed with my own eyes.

Leá's mother is Schizophrenic and Bipolar per her own accounts. Her brother (R.I.P.) had a mood disorder, and she also has a sister with Bipolar Disorder. So, Leá has always had experience with having mentally ill people around. Having that example to monitor makes it so much easier to identify within yourself, even if you aren't sure what it is. These facts must've helped Leá get through her teenage years.

At a young age Leá was labeled as a "Troubled Teen," no one gave her a chance or tried to figure out what was making her brain tick. I am quite sure if you asked her father he'd have a different account of events though. She claims to have had a very hard time in her home growing up. That is was a cold home, a very unsupportive one. She claims that she heard things like, "She is just like her mother" and "She can't be from our family." These comments had to have broken her young heart. If they in fact happened.

At age 12 Leá proved that misfortunate doesn't discriminate based on age. Her and her brother snuck out of the house and went to a party. This party changed Leá for the rest of her life. At this party her virginity was taken by a boy that didn't understand that NO means NO. This left Leá scared, hurt, and confused. Yet, when she reached out to her mother she was told that her being raped was her own fault, she shouldn't have snuck out. This had to have been like a stab in the throat, a devastating experience that was just made a little worse.

Once she was taken to the doctor she found out that her rapist had given her scabies along with a S.T.D. called Trichomoniasis. Not only did she have to live with what happened she had to be reminded of it every day as she treated the medical issues he had given her.

By her mid teen years Leá was starting to swing between manic and depressed monthly-which led her to self-medicate by her late teens. In contrast with statistics, Leá was not and is not promiscuous-per her own account. I do not know if I fully agree with that statement as she cheated on my brother several times during their relationship. Plus, being promiscuous is a common trend among Bipolar women. By 16 she claims she had also been institutionalized three times, once without her mother being able to be located. At this point they still didn't have an answer as to what was going on with her.

Through her 20's Leá never received a diagnosis, but her symptoms didn't go away and never eased. She had these extended episodes of mania followed by extended episodes of depression, it had to be mentally exhausting. She spoke of splurge shopping with no memory of where her money went and of days without the need to sleep. She said that her mother used to tell her that manic stages are like, "Burning bright like a star, then you burn out in one second."

There were a few changes by this time though, Lea was married to her first husband, a man that she would remain married to throughout her relationship with my brother. Early into their marriage the two of them bought a bar (coincidently at this same time her alcohol addiction worsened), and she became a mother. I can only imagine that she cheated on her husband and became pregnant seeing as though the child is openly not his child. I do not know that for a fact, she did not address it in the interview. Her cheating on him is just a story that my family has told me.

She likes to talk about how important her children are. Yet as time moved on it became clear that talking was about them was all she was willing to do when it came to her kids. By her mid 20's she'd taken to running out for days at a time and not being able to clearly explain where she was or what she was doing when she returned. She also became prone to bouts of violence when she was manic. All per her own accounts. Now, she was still undiagnosed and unmedicated so she had to do this all on her own. Live everyday figuring out how to cope without guidance.

Once Leá hit her early 30's she'd had enough, she knew something was wrong with her, she was tired of running away from it. She went manic one day and just left, she never looked back. She didn't take her daughter with her when she went. She left her with her husband, who, again, was not the child's father. He raised the little girl the best he knew how.

Once she could talk to a therapist she was properly diagnosed with Bipolar Disorder and Social Anxiety Disorder. She was prescribed Lithium but doesn't take it right. According to my brother while they were together she regularly quit taking her meds for extended periods of time and lied to him about taking them. This is a one-sided statement. If she was taking her meds- the doses needed and still do need to be adjusted. Leá had expressed that the medication helps her control her mood swings easier, it helps her think, makes it where she can work- when she takes it- I never saw evidence of these claims; I saw more evidence of what my brother claimed about her medication habits.

The truth about us is that she met my baby brother a few years back and I instantly hated her. As far as Leá was concerned I would've done anything to get her out of his life, anything to turn the clock back and remove her from the picture. At that time, I was entirely unsure as to why I didn't like her. At one point, I thought it might have been out of fear that she would take my brother from me. It didn't take long for me to realize that this was not the case. I've realized it was because I knew that she hadn't taken care of her first child and I feared she'd have children with him. I couldn't bear to watch what would happen to any children they would have in her care.

As I feared, she became pregnant. I love my niece and nephew with all my heart but I feel for them as well. The kids were born around 15 months apart from each other so Leá was basically pregnant for 2 years straight. In that time, she was unable to take her medication and has since had a hard time obtaining it. The biggest problem isn't if she could obtain her medications or not; the biggest problem was that both her and my brother were self-medicating with heroin. To this day, she still uses as far as I know. She does not have custody of either child, her father and stepmother has them.

When my niece was 8 months old the most tragic thing happened- she got a hold of heroin and overdosed. A few months later her baby brother was born with opiates in his system. They both survived but were deemed unsafe in their parent's care. While the ordeal was going on with my niece my brother and her were less than upfront about what was going on. It took longer than it needed to for them to find out the problem. My brother was asleep when it happened, per both of their statements, that leaves my niece in her mother's care at the time. If she had spoken up and told the ER that she had gotten ahold of her "stash" then they wouldn't have had to wait for the blood work to have come back. Who knows what those precious minutes could've done. What difference they could've made. To this day, she still refuses to admit her fault in the situation with her daughter.

Soon after the children were taken from them her and my brother feel deeper into the grips of drug addiction. Ending up homeless, living in a tent and begging for money. There were claims of prostitution made by my brother and a lot of laws broken by them both. They had several opportunities to try again and were not able to. CPS gave her almost unlimited chances before they finally revoked her parental rights. The truth is, the two of them are toxic together. In some ways, it is a blessing that she doesn't have her hands on the kids and in others I see it potentially hurting those babies deeply that their parents aren't there.

As a result of the overdose their youngest daughter has Autism. It is unproven that the overdose caused her Autism but it is a widespread belief that it did. She changed after that happened. We all watched it unfold. She lost abilities that she previously had directly after it happened. I am positive that her mother couldn't have handled raising her with her disabilities. The grandparents that are raising them are doing a phenomenal job at it. They show those children love and stability every single day.

Bipolar Disorder isn't easy, it isn't simply "mood swings," and we can't simply "get over it." This disorder can send us into the perils of hell. It can cause us to act differently than we would've otherwise. Like it has done with my brother's ex-girlfriend. She has become the shell of a person, moving from one relationship to another-looking for a place to call home. A place that will accept her despite all her questionable decisions. In this case, it led to a deep drug addiction and 2 children that will wonder why their parents didn't raise them and a 3rd that already grew up without her mother. So, like I said- Bipolar Disorder isn't simply "mood swings" or something we can "get over." It is a disorder that affects families and communities. Being able to "get over it" is a pipe dream. That isn't how it works, trust me, we all wish it was.

Picture Courtesy of Bing Images

Ch 11

The Echo of My Heart is Heard in Hers:

Shelena's Story

(Indiana)

Shelena

You know those people that exude love? The ones that people gravitate towards whenever they walk into a room? The ones everyone wants to stand next to in hopes that part of their shine will rub off. This woman is one of those people. Shelena is tall (well- taller than me), with the most amazing eyes I have ever had the pleasure of memorizing. She is a timeless beauty with a heart of gold. For these reasons and many more I am forever grateful that Shelena is my friend. I am even more grateful that I get to be her big sister. In fact, she is one of the sisters that I spoke of finding out about finding out about when I was little.

Shelena was first diagnosed with Bipolar Disorder around the age of 15, though it was apparent there was something going on before that. At that time her mother described her mood as being like a light switch; it could change as easily as the flip of a switch, I'd have to agree- I thought she was a brat. I remember at one point she was asked to help set the table, out of nowhere she started screaming that she didn't care if they loved her and she didn't need them. Before running off to her room she threw a glass and shattered her mother's salt shaker.

It was evident early on that Shelena had major issue with criticism. The littlest thing said could result in her locked in her room for days. I was the same way growing up and still am at times. This trend followed her into adulthood. Another trend that followed her into adulthood is the yearning to read, to escape into another world, to shut this one out. There is a large percentage of Bipolar individuals that are drawn to the arts. Whether it be writing, reading, drawing, painting, etc. We are drawn to those areas in great numbers.

By her mid 20's Shelena was married and had 2 children, despite her life changes her head hadn't changed much. Over the next 8 years she had 2 more; 3 girls and 1 boy total. Just like my life, one of her children is Autistic- her middle daughter. As I learned early on, with Autism comes added responsibilities.

Shelena's children, plus a niece and nephew of mine

See, one of the added responsibilities is having more doctors' appointments. Shelena has a habit of becoming overly nervous before appointments and missing them. She starts to get ready and then something happens and she stops. It's as if she just turns off or someone hits pause. The biggest problem in this is that she doesn't call to reschedule the appointment citing "fear of the receptionist getting mad at her for rescheduling" as the reasoning. On top of that her marriage has been plagued with fighting, depression, mania, and impatience. She is married to an amazing man that has stood by her no matter what. There has been a lot of "no matter what's" too. He's not innocent though. He has caused his fair share of damage to my baby sister's psyche.

Shelena and her husband, Ken

In their marriage Shelena has done the following to or because of her husband:

-Got into a fight with him over their kids that turned into a screaming match. During which she slammed a bottle down on the table and sliced her finger open

-She got into a verbal altercation with her husband one night and punched him in his mouth for calling her names. The punch screwed his mouth up but hurt her hand more. She tore her hand wide open and had to be hospitalized, it left an awesome scar though

-Her mother was ticking her off especially bad one day and Shelena didn't know what to do. Feeling completely overwhelmed she tend what seemed right: She hit her husband upside the head with a skillet

A few years into their marriage Shelena felt that life was closing in on her. She spent many years cheating on her husband with various men. I have always believed that she hated the fact that she was doing this but was unable to stop herself while she was in the act. I also believe that she was extremely unhappy at this point of time in her life. In the end, she filed for divorce. Many of us believe that she did this as a way of changing things up, a way of trying to get herself out of a funk. In that time, she met and started dating a boy that I grew up with. He is not a favorite person of mine. She also fought with her ex-boyfriend regularly. Shelena is a hard person to live with, as am I.

I can recall one instance when her (ex) boyfriend told her that it didn't really look like she cleaned that day. She instantly snapped. How dare he say that?! She proceeded to knock all the pictures off the wall, kicked a hole in the wall and lock herself in her room for hours. Locking herself in her room is Shelena's M.O. She does it anytime she becomes overwhelmed or falls into a deep depression. It is a defense mechanism that she takes to the extreme.

When you catch Shelena in a depressive stage you'll be meeting a completely different person, if you can catch her that is- more likely than not you'll never even get her to the door or on the phone. She cuts everybody out when she is like that. The only time in the woman's life that she annoys me is when she's depressive. Getting her out of bed is impossible. When Shelena locks herself up we all hold our breath, waiting for her to hit that sliding slope backwards in her Bipolar.

Calling what she does when she flips depressive a sliding slope is an understatement. I have never seen anybody in my life react to depression and stress the way that Shelena does. When she slips, it tends to be more like falling off a cliff. She falls hard. These extreme reactions have not only impacted her and her significant other's lives, it has affected her children's lives as well. On multiple occasions Shelena's children have been placed with family members or in foster care due to her house being dirty or because she failed a drug test. I had taken her Autistic daughter into my home on multiple occasions because of these reasons. I do not write about this to shame my sister. I write about it to show other sufferers that may have been through the same thing that going through stuff like that doesn't have to define you. It didn't define Shelena. She pushed on and bettered herself. It just took her a little time to get there. When they are adults her children will see that she pushed on and admire her for it. She has now been clean for several years. I couldn't be prouder of her.

Her episodes of depression can last anywhere up to 6 months. During that time, I am serious, no phone will be answered- no texts sent back. She doesn't leave her house for any reason, it's as if she disappeared. For a little while now she has been doing much better with it, she seems to be merging back into one person from two halves. The violence, small bout with drug abuse, and her promiscuity are very common for people like us. She is still working on getting past her habit of cutting though. It's been 5 years since she last did- but she still thinks about it. She's developed some coping strategies, if you will. You can see the coping strategies working in her everyday life in the areas of self-harm, patience, and love. In fact, to all our surprise, 2 months ago, I stood and witnessed her and her husband remarry in a church of God. I smiled ear-to-ear that day. I love my brother-in-law. He compliments her well.

When she goes into a slump he is there for her. He doesn't always react the correct way to her but he tries. Whenever she says that she feels like she needs to cut, he gets out his tattoo equipment. As you will hear from many people with Bipolar Disorder, they use tattoos and piercings to supplement. He helps her with this need. Shelena also likes to dig her fingernails into her hand/wrist until it bleeds a little too. He always encourages her to find another way to handle the pain.

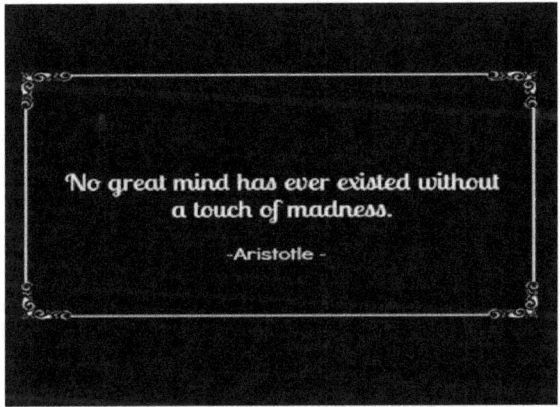

Shelena has had many misdiagnosis, as has many of us. At age 22 she was seen again by a therapist and re-diagnosed as Bipolar2 with comorbidities including BPD, Anxiety Disorder, and PTSD. Now came the hard part, it was time to commence the race to finding the right medication. I can tell you this, her medication history reads almost as if you picked up a pharmaceuticals book and started reciting from the "screwed in the head" section.

Medications Tried:

-Lexapro

-Effexor

-Wellbutrin

-Zoloft

-Trazodone

-Abilify

-Xanax

-Risperdol

-Seroquel

-Remeron

-Ambien

-Celexa

-Cymbalta

-Paxil

-Prozac

It must be said that Shelena probably wouldn't be as disturbed as she is if her paternal family (some of them-not all of them) had been a little less judgmental and a lot more accepting.

Despite his consistent effort to make up for it now, her father was quite absent in her life growing up. He wasn't there in the way a father should be. It was hard to see that when she was younger because she was daddy's girl; as she aged though his actions brought the issue to light. As she developed her own sense of self her father developed a hatred for it. They began to butt heads regularly. Eventually he stopped coming around (which had long been his M.O.). When he did come around it was for no good reason.

Shelena's children

Since her last child was born he's tried to make amends with her, with all his children and serious props need to be given for the effort. It seems though that his efforts only extend to the children that he provided a biological link to, not their children. He doesn't see Shelena's children, he rarely asks about them. There are not pictures of them hung in his home. For a few of us his efforts are good enough, for a few there'll never be enough "I'm sorries." I don't know if Shelena will ever fully forgive him but she is trying.

Another cause of torment for Shelena is her family and their inability to grasp what Autism is. They act as if her daughter being behind is a reflection on her ability to parent instead of the things she is doing being a common issue for Autistic children. This is a common issue in the Autism community. Our families just don't "get it." I experienced the same with my son and still do on many levels. In Shelena's case, the only way her daughter's Autism has reflected on her mothering abilities is positively. The progress my niece has made should be contributed to Shelena alone. I know how hard it has been for her, helping an Autistic child learn is one of the hardest yet rewarding tasks a person could take on and my sister has done it flawlessly.

Shelena and myself, in Seattle, Washington

Shelena is proof that you can take pure madness and turn it into pure perfection, if you have enough willpower. She shows that resolve can help you climb mountains that patience can aid you in helping a child blossom and that never giving up can inspire more people than imagined. She's a great mother and a great wife; as a sister- I couldn't ask for better.

Her world was a mess,
so she lost herself in
a wonderland of madness.

Picture Courtesy of Google Images

Ch 12

A Beautiful Disaster in the Making:

Ann's Story

(Indiana)

Ann was born into a family with the weirdest dynamics I have ever seen. Into a family that I almost was part of. In my opinion, the difference between where I could've been and where I am is literally 5 seconds. Looking at the daddy issues that have developed in all of her sisters I'd say it's a big 5 seconds. The 5 sisters have the most twisted concept of family which stems back to her paternal source. Of the 5, 4 openly admit having Bipolar Disorder.

Ann's 4 older sisters all have different relationships with her father.

-The oldest: Does not acknowledge him as her father because she was given up for adoption as a baby

-The 2nd sister in line was also adopted out-she won't have anything to do with any of the girls.

-The middle sister: she was always a daddy's girl- until she was a teenager that is. At that age, he distanced himself all while still criticizing her for how she is

-The sister right above Ann (in age) apparently has no mental disorders or any disorders otherwise. She lives away from the rest of the family

-Then there's Ann sitting there since age 13- feeling confused, lied too, and ignored; even if every bit of it is in an ill-fated attempt to protect her.

At 17 Ann is just now starting to find out who she is, who her family is, and who her parents are. As if 17 wasn't hard enough for a teenager Ann must add to it that most of the things she's been told about her sisters, her family- is a façade, a fake. An elaborate story concocted by her parents.

Most people at least know who is and who is not their sibling as they are growing up. You know, they know who is from who and why everybody's lives were the way they are. Ann didn't have that luxury, she was never given the option. Over the years, I've found that finding truth about the past in her house is much like trying to find a toothpick in a pile of hay- it's near impossible. I always knew this but had always hoped I was wrong. The oldest sister and middle sister were first allowed around Ann 5 or 6 years ago. They'd long been trying to get to know her but had been given no contact with her. The middle sister offered the bridge to Ann that the oldest sister had been looking for. She relayed messages back and forth and helped them get to know each other.

Once around each other for the first time Ann seemed so shy, so confused. In fact, she still is this way. Her behavior baffled her sisters greatly. Come to find out, she had no idea what was going on. The middle sister didn't realize the extent of the lies Ann had been told, neither did the oldest sister. At that time, she had no idea how the oldest even fit into the puzzle. She was confused. Her confusion wasn't easily soothed given the fact that her middle sister informed the oldest that their father had given a set of rules by which they had to follow to be in Ann's life. They tried desperately to obey him but in the end his mouth, their lack of respect, and those rules destroyed it.

Rules Given in Order for Ann's Sisters to be Part of her Life:

-The mothers of the sisters couldn't be mentioned in any form. This included to Ann and/or her mother

-No mention any of my other siblings besides us 5 girls

-No one could tell her his age when the oldest was born

-No one could speak to her about the adoptions

-No one could speak about the sister's (adopted) fathers

-We couldn't speak about growing up

-We couldn't speak ill of him or his wife at all

-All communications between her and her sisters were subject to monitoring

-His mother couldn't be spoken of

-The sisters couldn't talk in depth about their Bipolar Disorder

-Talking about drugs, alcohol, or sleeping around was off limits

-She couldn't go anywhere with her sisters or stay at their houses without him there too

They reported that it felt like they were being asked to hide every aspect of their lives. Anything that had occurred because he ran out was off limits. It felt like they were further lying to Ann about a piece of her sisters. It was now that they began to wonder what life inside that house was like for her. If she was this sheltered over things that she was going to eventually find out, then how do they treat her concerning friends or school? Getting closer to Ann answered those questions for her sisters and gave her sisters a relationship with the greatest 17-year-old on the face of this planet.

Her father is incredibly controlling. Like beyond controlling. When the middle sister's mother was married to him she used to have to take pictures of the vacuum patterns on the carpet after he left for work so that she could duplicate said marks before he got home. If she didn't do so then they wouldn't be allowed to step foot on that carpet. In Ann's life, the controlling behavior just worsened.

At 17 she has yet to hold a long-term job because he won't approve of any of them. It appears that her mother lives in fear under her own roof as well. I certainly hope I am wrong about this but given some of the stories I have been told by the sisters I almost guarantee I am spot on with that assumption.

For some time now Ann has asked her parents for help for her mental illness, begged even. There's obviously something wrong, her sisters are Bipolar and they suspect her father is as well. None the less they continuously ignored/ignore her pleas. They say that her being mentally ill as an impossibility; sometimes sinking as low as to ignore her all together. Acting like she never asked for the help she craves.

A few months back Ann overdosed in a failed attempt to commit suicide. This was after her older sisters begged for her parents to help her. They told them the stuff she was going through; her mother seemed very perceptive, her father was not. He shot down everything that was said and refused to believe that anything could be wrong with his youngest daughter. Living in a alternative reality mustn't be easy.

The night of the overdose she texted her oldest two sisters and her best friend to say goodbye and that she was sorry. It was a hard and frightening text to wake up to, I am sure. Her best friend got the text first and called the ambulance. Her parents were woken up in the middle of the night by sirens. They had no idea she was in her room trying to die.

She was sent to a facility for treatment. Even in this desperate situation her father argued with the hospital about if she needed help or not. I do not believe the gravity of the situation actually hit him that day. They had to threaten her parents with CPS to get her help. All of Ann's sisters were furious at the reaction of her parents to her suicide attempt.

The help that the hospital provided Ann would be for not once she was released. She was admitted into an inpatient psychiatric hospital out of state for one week because her parents were threatened if she wasn't put in the facility that legal measures would be taken. She was then allowed to start on medications but anytime raising the dose was mentioned the notion was shot down. We all know that the initial dose of any medication is not going to be the therapeutic dose; apparently, all of us but her parents know this fact.

Ann was also allowed to participate in therapy for around 4 months after her overdose before that was rejected too. Since all of her appointments have been cancelled. No follow-up counseling has been offered.

Lack of funds for a copayment is cited as the reasoning behind his actions. Not that the therapy sessions helped her all that much seeing as though the therapist required a parent be in the room during sessions. This made it near impossible for Ann to confide in her therapist about anything she needed to. To me, the reasons given for discontinuing the help she so obviously needs are sad excuses. I truly believe parents like that should be ashamed of themselves. Their dismissiveness could one day come at a great cost.

Her school life wasn't any easier than her home life. It is reported that teachers at school frequently had to redirect her due to her inability to focus. Luckily, in the last few months Ann has graduated early. School wasn't the only place that her Bipolar Disorder showed its ugly head though. Her friends tell her of things she's done and she doesn't clearly remember, and even her parents tell her that her mood and behavior is all over the place (yet refuse to believe she has any disorder.) It seems to me that she has the same things going on with her that they were trying to keep her from knowing about her sisters. Maybe if they could've been there more they would've been able to help her through it.

Ann's Bipolar Disorders presents quite erratically. She's plagued with bouts of mania, depression, and psychosis.

Ann's Bipolar Disorder Presents with:

-Impulsivity

-Mania

-Dysphoric Depression

-Hazy memory

-Psychosis

-Sleep Disturbances

-Issues with Focusing

-Anger

Psychosis in a 17-year-old is rare but not unheard of. I remember Ann telling me of times when she had a friend at her house and woke up in the morning to a scared friend, a headache, and very little memory of the night before. Her friend filled her in fast though. Apparently, Ann had started beating her head against the wall continually conveying she was hearing screams from behind her. Saying that the damn walls were moving on her. Ann also reports seeing dark shadow creatures moving around. These are often symptoms of BPD but sometimes can be reported with Bipolar Disorder.

Her stages of mania are quite impulsive, reminds me of myself when I was younger honestly. There was a time when Ann had everyone petrified because she was nowhere to be found. She had taken off with a few friends to let loose in an abandoned home that they frequented. Once in the house her and her friends realized there were gallons of paint in there being used for nothing. The first thought in her mind was to dance and play in the paint, so, they all went out into the street and poured the paint all over themselves. After doing so it occurred to her that they were going to have to walk home, in the heat, covered in paint then explain where she'd been, how said paint got on her, and why she hadn't been able to be reached for so long. At the same time, Ann was thinking these things her mother was driving around town searching for her.

This poor girl has nights where she sits up reading because her brain will not allow her to sleep, she has days where she wants to be awake but all her body will allow her to do is sleep. All she wants is an answer that helps her define herself as a woman, a human, and some pills that'll work. At this point, all she has is two parents making her feel crazy and a life that she can't possibly understand because she doesn't have all the pieces to her puzzle. It's hard to work a puzzle if half the pieces seem to come from a different box.

Ann's journey with mental illness is just now starting, she's only filled a few pages in her "book of crazy" but I have faith that she'll have enough material in a few years to write one hell of a book. I don't worry as much about her now as I do her in the future, as an adult. Once her father doesn't have complete control anymore and she finds out the things she still doesn't know she may have a hard time coping. On top of that, I wonder if once she's an adult she'll be able to forgive them for their dismissals and for ruling her with an iron fist. I often wonder if she'll move on and start over without looking back?

Will she choose the path which allows her to forget her past and moves towards her future? You know, the path that gives her a second change, a redo if you will. I'd like to think that's the road she'll take; the one I'd never be able to, the one that requires expressing forgiveness for another's wrongs against you?! She was born to be a rebel, to stand out, to paint the town. She is here to be heard and to love. Now all she must do is learn to live with herself in comfort, to embrace her mental disorder.

There's a bit of irony in this though. To be Bipolar is to sometimes bury your emotions inside until you explode. Being able to forgive for what she's been through as of now and what she is going to go through as she ages would be resplendently un-Bipolar like of her when thought about. I have high hopes for Ann in every path in life. I can't wait to watch her grow into an adult and start a life of her own. I can't wait to be able to call her my beautiful disaster and my friend.

The Mad Hatter:

Have I gone mad?

Alice:

I'm afraid so. You're entirely bonkers. But I'll tell you a secret. All the best people are.

Ch 13

Bipolar Disorder isn't just for Women

As mentioned before, there are no two Bipolar individuals that present the same way. Some are more pre-dispositioned towards violence; some depression; some sway towards mania; some towards their own personal hell. The stigma put on us Bipolar personalities is largely unfair and inaccurate. Granted the women in this book all, including myself, lean more towards the spectrum of madness: not all Bipolar individuals are insane.

Not all Bipolar individuals are women either. There are several Bipolar men in my life, all with different dispositions. How about children? There are children out there suffering through this disorder daily. Some of these children belonging to friends of mine, one of them is my little sister.

Bipolar Disorder in Men

During Manic episodes' men tend to present with:

-Hyperactivity

-Acting impulsively

-Difficulty concentrating

-Racing thoughts

-Inflated self-opinions

-Excessive talking

-Lessened need for sleep

-Increased risk of substance abuse

(Health)

All of which present significantly more severely than in women, in most cases. Not to mention men are less likely to get help for their disorder. Either they don't want to or can't admit that there is something wrong with them. In cases of the latter it tends to weigh heavily on family members. (Health)

During Depressive Episodes Men tend to present with:

-Feeling sad or "empty"

-Feeling hopeless, irritable, anxious, or angry

-Loss of interest in work, family, or once-pleasurable activities, including sex

-Feeling very tired

-Not being able to concentrate or remember details

-Not being able to sleep, or sleeping too much

-Overeating, or not wanting to eat at all

-Thoughts of suicide, suicide attempts

-Aches or pains, headaches, cramps, or digestive problems

-Inability to meet the responsibilities of work, caring for family, or other important activities

-Substance abuse

(Health)

When it comes to suicide and Bipolar Disorder, it's said that women are more likely to attempt to kill themselves but that men more likely to succeed. They must live with people looking at them as if their disorder is a reflection on the type of man they are. It's almost as if their Bipolar Disorder is being judged as a character flaw or a sign of weakness. (Ho)

Of the Bipolar men that I know it seems that the feeling of injustice in every encounter in life is strong. They feel as though everything that is said is a criticism of them and a stab at their manhood. Their episodes of Mania tend to heavily include the unaccountable spending of money and a lot of placing blame on other people for their actions. Living with a Bipolar man, that I have observed, is a hard endeavor to take on. They self-sabotage frequently. Where women tend to want reassurance in their illness, men tend to want the existence of their disorder to be erased. While being extremely loving people on their good days, they also harbor the potential to explode at a moment's notice and remain in that angered mood for long periods of time.

Let's look at some studies though.

Per (Izabela Kawa, 2005) most gender comparisons (of Bipolar cases) show no evidence of differences. They did report in this study of 121 women and 90 men that men more often than women reported mania at the onset of Bipolar I. It is also reported that men have higher rates of "comorbid alcohol abuse/dependence, cannabis abuse/dependence, pathological gambling and conduct disorder." Per this study, men were also more likely to report violence and outbursts with their Bipolar Disorder. The men also suggest that they find it more impossible to hold a conversation during episodes of mania. As opposed to women who reported higher rates of comorbid eating disorders, and weight change. Women also reported higher incidents of appetite change and insomnia during depression. Their conclusion in this study was that men and women were largely similar in their symptom presentation, age of onset of Bipolar Disorder, and in the total number of mood episodes. However, differences were noted in the type of episode at onset and comorbidity patterns.

A long-term study in England further pointed out the differences in how men and women present with Bipolar Disorder. In said study they took the gender differences in, "age at onset and incidence of first-episode mania and Bipolar Disorder in an epidemiological catchment area in southeast London over a 35-year period." This study used all adult cases, including their first-episode psychosis, mania, or hypomania, in Camberwell, southeast London from 1965–1999. These cases were identified and a "computerized diagnoses for the cases were generated by using the Operational Checklist for Psychotic Disorders program." With this program, they were able to calculate "incidence rates and rate ratios of DSM-IV Bipolar I disorder using their first manic episode categorized by gender and age." The differences in their ages at onset and of their first-episode of mania were noted. Their conclusion was that women had higher incidence rates of Bipolar I Disorder throughout adult life. It was noted that men appear to have an "earlier onset of mania and Bipolar Disorder than women." (Noel Kennedy, 2005)

Just as the above-mentioned studies suggest, substance abuse is a key problem for any person suffering from Bipolar Disorder. The problem seems to afflict men more heavily than it does women. There was a study that came out of the Stanley Foundation Bipolar Network. This study proves that in the that a full 49% of the men studied suffered from alcoholism; when that is compared to the near 29% of the women with Bipolar Disorder in this study that met the criteria for lifetime alcoholism you begin to see how large the difference in affliction it. Alcoholism in this study was associated with a history of polysubstance use in women with Bipolar Disorder and was associated with a family history of alcoholism in men with Bipolar Disorder. As stated in the study, "the magnitude of these gender-specific differences is substantial and warrants further prospective study." (Mark A. Frye, 2003)

Another key difference worth mentioning between onset of Bipolar Disorder in men and women is the increased chances of men with Bipolar Disorder having cardiovascular issues. It was determined diagnoses of cardiovascular disease (CVD) and CVD-related conditions differed by psychiatric diagnosis. The men used in the said study were male Veterans Administration patients from the mid-Atlantic region. There were 7,529 patients used in this study. Their average age was 54.5 years. At the conclusion of the study the prevalence of diagnoses ranged from 3.6% increase of a stroke to 35.4% increase in hypertension among men with Bipolar Disorder. When they compared those numbers to male Schizophrenia patients, they found that those with Bipolar Disorder were "19% more likely to have diabetes, 44% more likely to have coronary artery disease, and 18% more likely to have dyslipidemia." (Amy M. Kilbourne, 2007)

Children can be Bipolar too

When I found out a friend of mines son is Bipolar I was literally shocked, at a loss for words. I didn't know that it was possible for a child of that age to be diagnosed with Bipolar Disorder. Apparently, it is possible and the diagnosis can come as early as 6 years of age. (WebMd) My first thought was how does a parent handle that, my second was how does a child handle that?

According to NIMH 10 million Americans are diagnosed with Bipolar Disorder and more than half of those cases are individuals between the ages of 15-25. (Illness) The reason the age is set at 15 is because, while it can present in childhood, it's more likely to present in the mid-teens. Overall though, it's reported, that 2.2 percent of teenagers are diagnosed with Bipolar Disorder. (Illness)

Bipolar Disorder doesn't only affect adults, it also impacts the lives of our youth. While the disorder can be diagnosed in childhood it's difficult to do so. Mostly because the present diagnostic manual of mental disorders doesn't recognize childhood Bipolar Disorder, therefore meaning there's no official symptom criteria. (John Grohol) This condition in children has only recently been recognized as a legitimate diagnosis. The mania of Bipolar Disorder also tends to mirror

ADHD in children. This often leads to the use of the wrong medications and the wrong therapies.

According to leading studies, "when you look at available studies and available data they strongly suggest that prepubertal childhood BPD and Bipolar Disorder are non-episodic, chronic, rapid cycling, mixed manic states. They may be comorbid with attention-deficit/hyperactivity disorder (ADHD) and conduct disorder (CD). They may also demonstrate features of ADHD and CD, further obscuring recognition and consequent treatment." (Wanda K Mohr, 2001)

The signs of Bipolar Disorder in children are different than those in adults. When observing a child for Bipolar Disorder therapist often look for the following.

Signs and Symptoms of Mania in Children:

Mood Changes

-Overly silly or joyful mood (unusual for your child)

-An extremely short temper and unusual irritability

Behavioral Changes

-Sleeping little but not feeling tired

-Talking a lot and having racing thoughts

-Having trouble concentrating or paying attention

-Jumping from one thing to the next (in an unusual way)

-Talking and thinking about sex more often than usual

-Behaving in risky ways more often

-Seeking pleasure a lot

-Doing more activities than usual

-Hallucinations and Delusions

-Being a Daredevil

(NIMH, Bipolar Disorder in Children and Adolescents)

Signs and Symptoms of Bipolar Depression in Children:

Mood Changes

-Feeling extremely sad or hopeless

-Being in an irritable mood

-No longer interested in activities that were once enjoyed—hobbies, sports, friendships

Behavioral Changes

-Sleeping too much, hardly ever or trouble falling asleep

-Moving slowly or restlessness

-Changes in appetite or weight

-Little to no energy

-Problems concentrating

-Aches and pains for no reason

-Recurrent thoughts or talk of death or suicide

A study out of NSCB Medical School in Jabalpur, Madhya Pradesh reveals that pediatric mania seldom presents with a euphoric mood as it does in adults. They report in this study that the onset of Bipolar Disorder has been reported in children as young as 5 years; however, in India the youngest report is of a 6-year-old girl. In said study the speak of a 9-year-old boy from India whose parents brought him in begging for help with him. In the study the researchers report that the "patient started having decreased sleep (total duration reduced to 4-5 hours with early awakening at around 4 am in morning). Parents also noticed a change in his behavior, like increased activities. His sleep decreased and he started cleaning his room 6 a.m. in morning. He was playing with his dog saying that this is a tiger and i am a hunter. He started throwing utensils out of the kitchen saying that these are of no use and I will buy new ones for you. He was excessively talkative continuously singing like "mummy laal hain, papa neele hain, bade papa me current hai" etc. He was talking with lots of gestures, making faces and moving his hands in air. When his parents tried to send him to school, he said he doesn't need education as he is a hunter. There was no history suggestive of any organic illness, depressed mood, or any schizophrenic symptoms or substance abuse. The past history and family history were negative for any psychiatric illnesses. On mental status examination, his mood was predominantly elated, psychomotor activity was increased, the tone, tempo and volume of speech were increased, with pressure of speech at times. Delusion of grandiosity was present. All investigations like routine haemogram, urine examination, CT scan and an EEG revealed no abnormality. A diagnosis of first-episode mania was made and the patient was put on Valproic acid 300 mg BD, risperidone 3 mg and olanzapine 5 mg/day dose. Patient developed EPS with incontinence on 2nd day and his risperidone was reduced to 1 mg/day and olanzapine was removed. Patient showed significant improvement in 10 days and was advised to continue same treatment for 15 days until subsequent follow-up." This study closes by stating that "children with mania may be relatively uncommon in outpatient settings, but clinical practice suggests that they may account for a substantial number of childhood psychiatric hospitalizations and manifest with chronic psychosocial disability." (Swapnil Agrawal, 2016)

There is one more group of individuals that Bipolar Disorder impacts that are often forgotten. One day every single one of us will fit into this category, whether Bipolar or not. I am talking about the most respected members of society; our elderly.

Bipolar Disorder in the Elderly:

Right now, near 12% of the U.S. population is 65 years or older. Bipolar Disorder doesn't disappear as you age. It is still ever present in the elderly, it is just way too understudied and often overlooked. The fact that it was widely undiagnosed before the 1980s also suggests that there could be individuals that are misdiagnosed and have carried said misdiagnoses into their later years.

It is estimated that by 2025 the percentage of elderly in our communities is expected to jump up to near 20%. A study published in the Psychiatric Annals points out that, "most all of the relevant published data about Bipolar Disorder in the elderly is related to late-life mania. There is little published data on the depressive episodes of older patients with Bipolar Disorder, or on the relationship between late-life depression and Bipolar Disorder. In addition, earlier research does not clearly distinguish primary Bipolar Disorder of late onset from secondary mania occurring in older individuals." (C Umapathy, Benoit H Mulsant, & Bruce G Pollock, 2000)

While most commonly Bipolar Disorder peaks either in adolescence or in early adulthood, some 10% of patients with Bipolar Disorder become ill for the first time after 50 years of age. Per the above-mentioned study, "in the general population, the lifetime prevalence of Bipolar Disorder has been estimated to decrease with age from 1.4% in young adults to 0.1% to 0.4% in those older than 65 years. A similar decrease with age in the lifetime prevalence of major depressive disorder has been reported. This paradoxical finding of a decrease in lifetime prevalence associated with increasing age has been attributed to several factors: a cohort effect postulating that younger generations are more susceptible to mood disorders; an increased mortality among patients with mood disorders, leading to their underrepresentation in older cohorts; or, more importantly, methodological problems in the definition, detection, and diagnosis of late-life mood disorders." (C Umapathy, Benoit H Mulsant, & Bruce G Pollock, 2000)

When you look at the incidents of mania and depression in elderly Bipolar patient's studies show that "(hypo)manic symptoms are not as frequent as depressive symptoms in the elderly. Approximately 5% of elderly Bipolar patient's experience (hypo)mania each year. It is not possible to draw firm conclusions on prevalence rates in communities, nursing

homes and other study samples because of limited data."
(Annemiek Dols1, 2011)

Treating elderly Bipolar patient's is a tad bit different than
treating a younger Bipolar patient. Studies suggest that, "lithium
is widely utilized in younger populations but has been found to
be largely un-tolerated in the elderly. Valproate semi sodium
and carbamazepine are widely prescribed compounds in older
adults with Bipolar Disorder. However, the popularity of these
compounds has occurred in context of an absence of evidence-
based data." (Martha Sajatovic, 2005)

The same study suggests that atypical antipsychotics have
"expanded the treatment armamentarium for Bipolar Disorder
in mixed populations and may offer particular promise in
management of Bipolar illness in older populations as well."

The typical atypical Antipsychotics that are used to treat Bipolar Disorder:

-Olanzapine

-Risperidone

-Quetiapine

-Ziprasidone

-Aripiprazole

These medications approved by the US FDA for the treatment of
Bipolar Disorder. The roadblock that doctors hit when treating
the elderly is that there are absolutely no published trials for
the use of these medications in elderly patients. That doesn't

mean that they aren't exploring this area though. Per (Martha Sajatovic, 2005), "preliminary reports on the use of clozapine, risperidone, olanzapine and quetiapine suggest a role for the use of these agents in late-life Bipolar Disorder. Information with ziprasidone and aripiprazole specific to geriatric Bipolar Disorder is still lacking."

Given the reliable data suggesting that individuals with Bipolar Disorder are at a higher risk of developing Alzheimer's I'd say that the research that will come out surrounding late onset Bipolar Disorder in the next few years will be very telling. I'm sure it's become clear by now that Bipolar Disorder can touch anyone from any walk of life at any age. It's written in our genes and in our homes, it's almost always determined before our births and made worse as we grow.

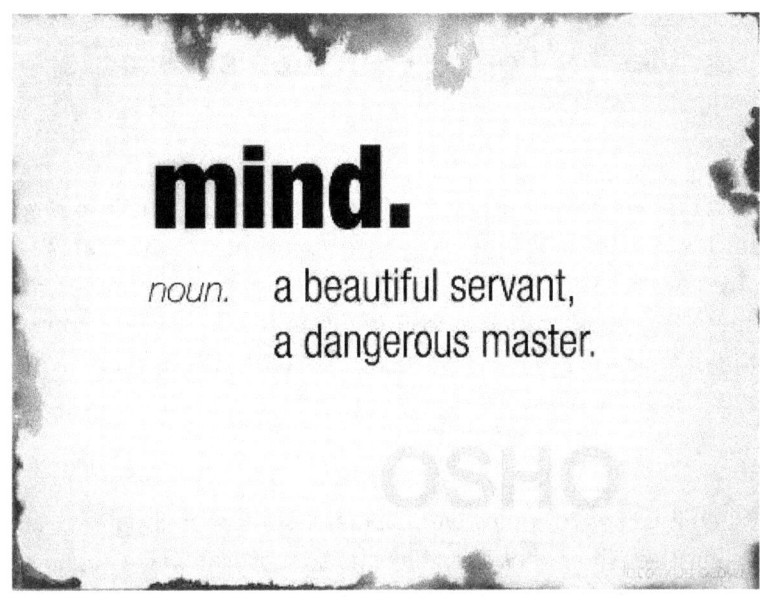

Picture Courtesy of Google Images

Ch 14

Advice for Coping with Bipolar Disorder

Now that we have touched on all the facts, myths, and inspiring stories of Bipolar Disorder let's have a look into a topic that is often overlooked. What do you do if your family just simply doesn't "get" what Bipolar Disorder is or how to help you cope with it? In contrast, let's also look at what our family members could do to help us cope.

When it comes to coping with Bipolar Disorder family is imperative. Their understanding and support can make all the difference. As I stated in previous chapters, even if they do not seem to "get" it- do not stop trying to explain to them what you need from them. It is also important to point out that even if they never "get it" that is no reason to give up on yourself or your healing. You can and will survive without their support, it is just nice to have it.

If you are a parent or family member of an individual with Bipolar Disorder, we know you are in a hard position. We are not easy people to understand and support, none the less, we still need your love. In my research, I went through many articles and studies about helping loved ones deal with Bipolar Disorder. I found one article that stood out to me above the rest. The author of said article was Ms. Natasha Tracey. I have decided to direct you to her advice to loved ones. Her advice not only embraces the things you could do to help your loved ones but also the things you should do to help yourself. She did a very good job writing the article. It is cited in the subtitle below. You should look her up.

Per (Tracey N. , 2008), she lists these important points of advice:

-Educating yourself is more important than you'd think.

As she states, "It is imperative that you seek out and learn all you possibly can about Bipolar Disorder. Like a General fighting a battle you are going to need all the ammunition you can garner at your disposal. There are many different sources of information...books, films, internet, support groups and others. Take from as many as you can and learn."

I would also add that you should ask your loved one with Bipolar Disorder what areas of their disorder they would like for you to learn about. As I have stated several times, no two people with Bipolar Disorder present their symptoms the same way. Your loved one may be more apt to fall into a depression as opposed to going manic. Knowing this is important for your research.

-Communication can be a game changer.

Ms. Tracey advises that you should, "Do all you can to keep communication lines open between you and your ill relative. Assure him you are there for him and that you know he is sick but will get well again. Try to be a part of his wellness, but not a part of his illness. Encourage every effort to get better and go with him, rather than send him for help if he wishes. Try to project positive thoughts about his recovery."

I love the line, "Try to be part of his wellness, but not a part of his illness." You will find that this is very relevant advice.

-Network for added support and help.

In this bit of advice Ms. Tracey's words couldn't be more accurate, "Lessen the burden on the family by broadening the network of people who can help in a crisis. Another person who has been through this, a concerned friend or professional may offer respite when you need it most...One of the hardest things for family members to do sometimes, but one of the most important. It is imperative that you realize that your life doesn't stop to revolve around your ill relative. Take care of your own health and your own needs or you may not have the strength to cope."

-Know your loved one's warning signs and triggers.

This is one of the most pertinent bits of advice I have seen. It is so easy to trigger an episode in a Bipolar person without intending to do so. Suicide Ideology is all too common in individuals with Bipolar Disorder.

Given the unpredictability of Bipolar Disorder, knowing the triggers is an important tool for helping your loved one heal as well. You should also prepare yourself for the possible reactions your loved one may have during a given episode; in case you accidentally do trigger them. Understanding ways to calm your loved one is important too, in case someone else triggers them.

-Don't Expect Too Much of Yourself

Ms. Tracey says it best when she says, "Surprise. Surprise. You are not superman (or woman) and there are limits to what you can handle. It is natural for your emotions to vary. You are dealing with a serious situation. It's natural to feel angry, frustrated, exhausted. These are valid feelings and ones shared by all families of Bipolar. So, cut a little kindness to yourself into the equation."

-Don't Blame Yourself

Another important point that Ms. Tracey brings up is that individuals with Bipolar Disorder have a chemical imbalance in their brains. They do and say things that there is no swaying them from doing and saying. In those moments, it is possible that you may be blamed for their actions, by them; or, that you may be blamed for their Bipolar Disorder all together. As Ms. Tracey suggests, don't listen to them! She suggests telling them that you know that their actions in that moment is just their illness talking. I would extend further advice that you only do that if you feel you have complete control over the situation. In some Bipolar individuals that may trigger them. It would me.

-Find somebody to talk to about your situation when you need to.

Ms. Tracey suggests that, "It is hard sometimes to talk to others about how out of control things have become in your life. You don't want gossip or pity - you don't want lasting stigma - but you do need to talk to someone. Find a self-help group in your area if there is one - if there isn't, start one. You'd be amazed at how many others face the same issue - or talk to a close friend."

-Don't ever give up.

Don't ever give up. It is OK to take a step back from a situation when you are feeling overwhelmed but remember that you are dealing with a person that you love and that wants to get well (hopefully). Ms. Tracey points out that, "Recovery from an episode is not often a straight path. Relapses are common. Wellness is achievable and has been achieved by many."

-Remember that there will be a next time.

As the article points out, "I know you don't want to hear this. But chances are very good that there will be another episode. Try to be prepared." The research you have done on Bipolar Disorder and the information you have absorbed concerning triggers and so forth will help you in the case of an episode. In case it is a bad episode, have a plan ready. In this plan make sure you have everything you need in the event that you may have to call for help. Per this article, "Have telephone numbers - doctor, emergency, admitting hospital, support, advice, etc., readily available. Ensure insurance is in place and the best that you can manage for psychiatric illness."

Ms. Tracey also suggests that you have an advanced directive in line for your loved one, in case an extreme situation presents itself. We all hope that will never happen but in life you never know what the next day will bring. Talking to your loved one about what they would want should they pass on will leave you with the ease of mind that you will represent them in death the way they would've wanted to be remembered.

(Tracey N. , 2008)

While knowing how to handle a loved one with Bipolar Disorder is important, there is a flipside to the issue. Many people with Bipolar Disorder have no idea how to "deal" with family and friends that have no clue how to handle our illness. This can add to our stress and promote arguing and emotional misconceptions; not to mention trigger episodes of mania and depression.

When dealing with non-supportive people in your life try to keep in mind that they may not fully understand what Bipolar Disorder is. It may not be a case of them not being supportive. Before you jump to conclusions make sure you have educated said individual about your illness. If you are in the presence of an individual that does not seem to "get it" no matter what you say or do, consider the following.

How to deal with unsupportive people in your life:

-Identify that some people will never "get it" and that this may well be one of those people.

Per an open letter published to the Huffington Post to people with mental illness, "Focus on your allies. Unsupportive people can stay on the shore while you sail into a cheesy postcard sunset. Don't take along any of their hurtful words because they slow your ship down. Let them fly off the back. Only kindness is allowed on board." (Griffin, 2015)

-Work on your reactions when you are triggered.

Some people are always going to trigger you and it is impractical to think that you can avoid every single one of them all the time. Working on the reactions that you have whenever you are triggered in different ways will help you avoid uncomfortable situations and time spent questioning whether or not you acted inappropriately after the fact.

-Remain calm.

There are people out there that live to cause drama. Don't give them the power to dictate how you behave or how your day goes. Breathe when you feel overwhelmed, try to think before you speak. When you feel your anger boiling up, remove yourself from the situation, if possible.

-Avoid triggers.

As I already pointed out, it is unrealistic to believe that you can avoid all triggers all the time. You can however try to avoid situations where you foresee triggers arising.

-Protect your emotions.

I found an article from The Huffington Post that was for entrepreneurs but one bit of advice rang true for mental illnesses. The article stated, "There will be some people you are not willing to eliminate from your life. You have to handle them differently: Insulate. The insulation in a house doesn't eliminate the outside temperature, it just keeps it out of the house. That's what you have to do with the negativity and criticism you're receiving. You have to keep it out. When someone gives you resistance, remember No. 1 — they don't understand. Since they don't have the perspective you have, they can't possibly understand where you are coming from. What they say isn't relevant to you. Their statements are not for you." (Steinmann, 2015)

Picture by AmyYakimoff.wikispaces.org

Ch 15

There isn't a Single Thing We're Incapable of because "We're Bipolar"

As I previously stated, it was recently brought to my attention that there are people out there that think being Bipolar prevents one from being a parent or holding a job; that the diagnosis somehow means you cease to exist as a human. To my disbelief, I was recently subjected to treatment as such, as though I couldn't and shouldn't take care of children because of my diagnosis. Like I'm scum because my medical records have a few interesting pages in them, like a waste of time. The part that befuddled me the most was that the individual doing the judging has never met me, there was one phone conversation between the two of us before I was tossed into the "waste of time" pile and they proceeded to move on to the next person.

The point is, I was being judged based on words on paper not on my actual personality or ability. My children are my whole world, even when I'm having a manic episode or am stuck in a depression- they come first; my nieces and nephews are my heart- without them I'm nothing. I'd never hurt, ignore, or expose any of them to my crazy, implying that I would or could is insulting and makes me question your character harder than you're questioning my merit.

Part of treatment is working your way through and past unexpected triggers and anger. This situation has been a test for me, I have failed on some fronts and passed with flying colors on others. This disorder is always going to be a struggle, every single day; it's a struggle for everyone that has it whether they have Bipolar 1 or 2, whether it is Unipolar or Rapid, no matter what it's a struggle. It doesn't just happen to little girls or grown men in the middle of nowhere either. This disorder has been given some sense of reality lately because it also inflicts our rich and famous.

There are many people in the public eye that have been diagnosed with Bipolar Disorder, or are believed to have been. They live/lived their lives with a sense of control and grace, suffering privately alone.

<u>People in the Public Eye with Bipolar Disorder:</u>

-*Catherine Zeta Jones (actress)*

-*Demi Lovato (actress/singer)*

-*Britney Spears (singer)*

-*Kurt Cobain (musician)*

-*Marilyn Monroe (actress)*

-*Sinead O'Connor (singer)*

-*Vincent Van Gogh (painter)*

-*Carrie Fisher (actress)*

-*Virginia Woolf (writer)*

-*Linda Hamilton (actress)*

-*Ben Stiller (actor)*

-Sting (musician)

-Jim Carrey (actor/comedian)

-Jean-Claude Van Damme (actor/martial artist)

-Robin Williams (actor/comedian)

-Tim Burton (director/writer)

-Drew Carey (actor)

-Axl Rose (musician)

-Elizabeth Taylor (actress)

-Larry Flynt (entrepreneur)

(Unknown)

That is a simply inspirational list of people, both living and dead. Each of them with a myriad of accomplishments among them. Those people never let anything tell them they can't reach their dreams, and if they did they didn't listen to them for long. We could all take a lesson from them and one from every mentally ill person that comes your way. Only thing harder than living with a disability is living with an invisible one.

Being Bipolar inherently makes you more artistic. There is a case study out of The American Journal of Psychiatry that talks about this very thing. In said study the "rates of mental illness were examined in 30 creative writers, 30 matched control subjects, and the first-degree relatives of both groups." In conclusion, the study had shown that the writers had a "substantially higher rate of mental illness." I don't know how I personally feel about this finding but it's good to know. In addition, "There was also a higher prevalence of affective disorders and creativity in the writers' first-degree relatives, suggesting that these traits run together in families and could be genetically mediated. Both writers and control subjects had IQs in the superior range; the writers excelled only on the WAIS vocabulary subtest, confirming previous observations that intelligence and creativity are independent mental abilities." (Creativity and mental illness: prevalence rates in writers and their first-degree relatives, 2006)

here's
to
all
the
broken
people.

Ch. 16

Never Be Afraid to Seek Out Help: Important Information

As spoke about earlier in this book, suicide is a considerable problem and concern among the Bipolar community. It's so incredibly important to know the warning signs and triggers. Remember to always take a suicide threat or attempt seriously, always pay attention to your loved one's words. Always believe it could happen and may happen in your family so that you can work from the start to prevent it.

With Bipolar children and teens, you absolutely can't be too chary when it comes to this topic. We need to be watching our youth closely for signs and talking to them about their feelings regularly. Statistically people with early-onset Bipolar Disorder are at greater risk for attempting suicide than those whose symptoms start in adulthood. One study on Bipolar Disorder in children and teens found that more than one-third of the kids have made at least one serious suicide attempt to kill themselves. (NIMH, Bipolar Disorder in Children and Adolescents)

This fact about Bipolar Disorder in children has touched the life of a friend of mine. Her story is one that leaves you sitting there breathless trying to grasp how she still smiles, how she hasn't given up, how she is so remarkable. This woman's son is Autistic as well as Bipolar. Unfortunately, he's suicidal at times. A few years back she and her husband found their son hanging in his room, he hadn't died (what that matters I do not know) but part of her heart sure did.

This boy is the sweetest, brightest, terribly loving little boy- the drastic change in temperament is scary and shows how important it is to watch out for signs of suicide in any Bipolar child or adult in your life. Also, remember that some of the symptoms and signs can be experienced by a child without there being Bipolar Disorder present. The level of severity is what's key; that and therapy.

SUICIDE WARNING SIGNS:

Conditions and Situations that are Typically Associated with an Increased Risk of Suicide:

-The death or terminal illness of relative or friend

-Dealing with a divorce, separation, broken relationship, added stress on family

-A personal loss of health whether it's real or imaginary

-A loss of job, home, money, status, self-esteem, personal security

-Showing alcohol or drug abuse signs

-Exhibiting signs of depression

(Metanoia)

A younger person's depression may be masked by them seeming to be hyperactive or like they are acting out. In elderly people, it's sometimes incorrectly ascribed to the effects of aging. Whenever a person's depression seems to quickly disappear for no obvious reason it should become a cause to be concerned. The early stages of recovery from depression can be a high-risk period too. (Metanoia)

Emotional and Behavioral Changes Associated in People with a Heightened Risk of Suicide:

-A Deep Overwhelming Pain: a pain that may exceed the person's pain coping abilities

-A Sense of Hopelessness: things will never get better

-Feeling Completely Powerless: the feeling that one's resources both physically and with the inwardly are exhausted

-Feelings of Worthlessness: shame, guilt, self-hatred, feeling like no one cares; fears of losing control, of harming themselves or others.

-Personality Saddens: becoming withdrawn, tired, apathetic, anxious, irritable, or prone to angry outbursts.

-Diminishing Performance at School, Work, or Other Activities: occasionally the reverse

-Social Isolation: association with a group that has different moral standards than those of the persons

-A Declining Interest in Sex, Friends, or Activities Previously Enjoyed

-Neglect of Their own Personal Welfare: deteriorating physical appearance.

-Large Variations in Either Direction with Sleeping or Eating habits.

-Self-Starvation: dietary mismanagement, disobeying medical instructions (More Often with Older Individuals)

-Difficult Times: holidays, anniversaries; just before and after diagnosis of a major illness; just before and during disciplinary proceedings

(NIMH, What is Depression)

Suicidal Behavior:

-Of course, if there had been previous suicide attempts, even mini-attempts you should be concerned

-Being Blunt about it, explicit statements speaking of suicidal ideation

-The development of suicidal plan, acquiring the means to carry out the plan, rehearsal type of behavior

-Self-inflicted injuries, such as cuts, burns, or head banging are a large sign; typically, the injuries are where they can be hidden (forearms, upper legs, and the upper sides are popular locals)

-Exhibiting reckless behavior is also a concern

-If the person starts to make out or completes a will or begin to give away their favorite possessions there is a reason to be alarmed

- If their goodbye become quite inappropriate, like they'll never see you again there could be a problem

-They begin using verbal behavior that is ambiguous or indirect: examples: "I'm going away on a real long trip", "You won't have to worry about me anymore", "I want to go to sleep and never wake up", "I'm so depressed, I just can't go on", "Does God punish suicides?", "Voices are telling me to do bad things", ALSO: If they make requests for euthanasia information, engage in inappropriate joking, stories you should most likely be concerned.

(NIMH, What is Depression)

Depression:

Depression is often over looked or ignored, chalked up to someone being lazy. It is so much more than that. You lose all control yourself along with the ability to function. Depression is real, it is big, and it doesn't go completely away without help.

(NIMH, What is Depression)

Ways to get Help Locally:

-A mental health specialists; psychiatrists, psychologists, social workers, or mental health counselors

-A health maintenance organization

-Community mental health centers

-Hospital psychiatry departments and/or outpatient clinics

-Mental health programs at medical schools

-State hospital/outpatient clinics

-Family services, social agencies

-Peer support groups

-Private clinics

-Employee assistance programs

-Local medical and/or psychiatric societies

(NIMH, What is Depression)

You can also check the phone book under "mental health," "health," "social services," "hotlines," or "physicians" to find various phone numbers and addresses. If need be you could go to a hospital, if it is an emergency. The emergency room doctor can usually provide temporary help and provide you with the information about how to get further help. (NIMH, What Is Depression?)

Substance Abuse:

Bipolar and drugs are almost synonymous. Substance abuse is something that is close to my heart, not only was I an addict for a long time I have had several siblings with problems with drugs as well. I can't think of too many things in life that are harder than getting off drugs. One of the things that I can say for sure is harder is being the parent or sibling of someone that is addicted to drugs.

Behavioral Changes:

Being addicted to drugs negatively affects a person's behavior as they become more dependent on the substance.

The drug itself can:

-Alter your brain's ability to focus

-Affect your ability to form coherent thoughts

-Increased aggression

-Lethargy

Depression

-Sudden changes in friends

(Drugabuse)

Are you one of those people that aren't sure what is and what isn't an illegal drug? I know a lot of people like that. Whenever it is said that a person is a substance abuser it could me a few things.

Illicit Drugs:

-Alcohol

-Bath Salts

-Cocaine

-Crack

-Crystal Meth

-Ecstasy

-Heroin

-Inhalants

-Ketamine

-Marijuana

-Meth

-PCP

-Steroid

(Drugabuse)

Prescription Drugs:

-Adderall

-Alprazolam

-Ambien

-Ativan

-Clonazepam

-Hydrocodone

-Klonopin

-Lorazepam

-Methadone

-Opiates

-Oxycodone

-Oxycontin

-Percocet

-Suboxone

-Subutex

-Tramadol

-Valium

-Vicodin

-Xanax

(Drugabuse)

There are a few options for drug addicts that want to recover. There is always detox (which I firmly believe is a waste unless you also go through rehab), behavioral therapy, and outpatient and inpatient care facilities.

Individuals with Bipolar Disorder, just like individuals with any other mental illness, are just trying to make it through each day without incident. We don't mean to offend or snap, most of the time. We just want to be seen and to be heard; to be let know that the world hasn't forgotten us. We just have a bit of a different perspective of it.

Sources of Help:

-Suicide Prevention Lifeline

1-800-273-TALK (8255)

TTY: 1-800-799-4889

Website: www.suicidepreventionlifeline.org

-SAMHSA's National Helpline

1-800-662-HELP (4357)

TTY: 1-800-487-4889

Website: beta.samhsa.gov/find-help/national-helpline

-Disaster Distress Helpline

1-800-985-5990

TTY: 1-800-846-8517

Website: disasterdistress.samhsa.gov

-Behavioral Health Treatment Services Locator

Website: findtreatment.samhsa.gov

-Buprenorphine Physician & Treatment Program Locator

Website: buprenorphine.samhsa.gov/bwns_locator/

-Opioid Treatment Program Directory

Website: dpt2.samhsa.gov/treatment/

(Samhsa)

About the Author

Brooke is a 32-year-old author from Indiana. She's the mother of 2 beautiful little boys and she's been a wife for over a decade, they are her life, her passion. Brooke's the author that

 never knew she was an author. She's the mother that never thought she'd be a mother and the wife that never thought she'd be a wife.

Not only is her oldest son Autistic but she is Bipolar 2, both severe forms of their disorders. Through support groups and research, it's been possible for her to cope, now she wants to repay their generosity by hopefully helping another person with Bipolar Disorder understand what is going on with them.

Find more writings from Brooke Price at:

www.brookepricesbooks.weebly.com

http://insideofsomeoneelse.blogspot.com/

http://www.emaxhealth.com/user/12577/track

https://www.amazon.com/-/e/B00HUEEUYQ

References

(n.d.). Retrieved from Nimh.nih.gov.

(n.d.). Retrieved from Bipolar-lives.com.

(n.d.). Retrieved from dbsalliance.org.

(n.d.). Retrieved from webmd.com.

Amy M. Kilbourne, J. S. (2007). *Cardiovascular Disease and Metabolic Risk Factors in Male Patients With Schizophrenia, Schizoaffective Disorder, and Bipolar Disorder*. Retrieved from Sciencedirect.com: http://www.sciencedirect.com/science/article/pii/S0033318207710058

Annemiek Dols1, R. K. (2011, December). *Bipolar disorder in the elderly*. Retrieved from Future Medicine: http://www.futuremedicine.com/doi/full/10.2217/ahe.11.75

Babak Roshanaei-Moghaddam, M. W. (2015, Jan 15). *Premature Mortality From General Medical Illnesses Among Persons With Bipolar Disorder: A Review*. Retrieved from Psychiatry Online: http://ps.psychiatryonline.org/doi/full/10.1176/ps.2009.60.2.147

C Umapathy, M., Benoit H Mulsant, M., & Bruce G Pollock, M. P. (2000, July 1). *Bipolar Disorder in the Elderly*. Retrieved from Healio.com: http://www.healio.com/psychiatry/journals/psycann/2000-7-30-7/%7Bd38c51e3-3115-4bc3-9eea-af9b037da726%7D/bipolar-disorder-in-the-elderly

Creativity and mental illness: prevalence rates in writers and their first-degree relatives. (2006, April 1). Retrieved from The American Journal of Psychiatry: http://ajp.psychiatryonline.org/doi/abs/10.1176/ajp.144.10.1288

Diseases and Conditions: Bipolar Disorder. (n.d.). Retrieved from MayoClinic: http://www.mayoclinic.org/diseases-conditions/bipolar-disorder/basics/causes/CON-20027544

Donald M. Hilty, M. K. (1999, Feb 1). *A Review of Bipolar Disorder Among Adults.* Retrieved from Psychiatry Online: http://ps.psychiatryonline.org/doi/abs/10.1176/ps.50.2.201

Drugabuse. (n.d.). *Symptoms and Signs of Drug Abuse.* Retrieved from http://drugabuse.com: http://drugabuse.com/library/symptoms-and-signs-of-drug-abuse/

Elisabeth Dawson, E. P. (1995, April 25). *Linkage studies of bipolar disorder in the region of the Darier's disease gene on chromosome 12q23-24.1.* Retrieved from American Journal of Medical Genetics: http://onlinelibrary.wiley.com/doi/10.1002/ajmg.1320600203/full

Federman, R. (2014, Feb 13). *Misdiagnosis of Bipolar Disorder.* Retrieved from Psychology Today: https://www.psychologytoday.com/blog/bipolar-you/201402/misdiagnosis-bipolar-disorder

Genetics of bipolar disorder. (n.d.). Retrieved from The Journal of Medical Genetics: http://jmg.bmj.com/content/36/8/585.short

Griffin, R. (2015, Oct 15). *An Open Letter to a Person With Mental Illness*. Retrieved from HuffingtonPost.com: http://www.huffingtonpost.com/rachel-griffin/an-open-letter-to-a-person-with-mental-illness_b_8266846.html

Health, N. I. (n.d.). *Men and Depression*. Retrieved from http://www.nimh.nih.gov: http://www.nimh.nih.gov/health/publications/men-and-depression/index.shtml

Ho, D. (n.d.). *Symptoms of Bipolar Disorder in Men*. Retrieved from http://www.ehow.com: http://www.ehow.com/facts_5019516_symptoms-bipolar-disorder-men.html?ref=Track2&utm_source=ask

Illness, M. (n.d.). *Bipolar Disorder in Children and Teens*. Retrieved from http://www.nami.org: http://www.nami.org/Template.cfm?Section=By_Illness&template=/ContentManagement/ContentDisplay.cfm&ContentID=13107

Institute, L. (n.d.). *Bipolar Disorder*. Retrieved from www.brainexplorer.org: http://www.brainexplorer.org/bipolar_disorder/Bipolar_Disorder_Aetiology.shtml

Izabela Kawa, J. D. (2005, March 11). *Gender differences in bipolar disorder: age of onset, course, comorbidity, and symptom presentation*. Retrieved from Wiley Online Library: http://onlinelibrary.wiley.com/doi/10.1111/j.1399-5618.2004.00180.x/full

John Grohol, P. (n.d.). *Symptoms of Childhood Bipolar Disorder*. Retrieved from http://psychcentral.com:

http://psychcentral.com/lib/symptoms-of-childhood-bipolar-disorder/0001518

Kristalyn Salters-Pedneault, P. (2016, May 10). *What is Splitting?* Retrieved from verywell.com: https://www.verywell.com/what-is-splitting-425210

Lori L Altshulera, b. ,. (2000, July 16). *An MRI study of temporal lobe structures in men with bipolar disorder or schizophrenia.* Retrieved from ScienceDirect: http://www.sciencedirect.com/science/article/pii/S000 6322300008362

Mark A. Frye, M. L. (2003, May 1). *Gender Differences in Prevalence, Risk, and Clinical Correlates of Alcoholism Comorbidity in Bipolar Disorder.* Retrieved from The American Journal of Psychiatry: http://ajp.psychiatryonline.org/doi/abs/10.1176/appi.aj p.160.5.883

Martha Sajatovic, S. M. (2005, January). *Managing Bipolar Disorder in the Elderly.* Retrieved from SpringerLink: http://link.springer.com/article/10.2165/00002512-200522010-00003

McGrath, J. (n.d.). *Bipolar Disorder Overview.* Retrieved from health.howstuffworks.com: http://health.howstuffworks.com/mental-health/mental-disorders/bipolar-disorder5.htm

Metanoia. (n.d.). *What can I do to help someone that may be suicidal.* Retrieved from www.metanoia.org: http://www.metanoia.org/suicide/whattodo.htm

NIMH. (n.d.). *Bipolar Disorder in Children and Adolescents.* Retrieved from http://www.nimh.nih.gov:

http://www.nimh.nih.gov/health/publications/bipolar-disorder-in-children-and-adolescents/index.shtml

NIMH. (n.d.). *What is Depression.* Retrieved from http://www.nimh.nih.gov: http://www.nimh.nih.gov/health/publications/depression/index.shtml#pub9

Noel Kennedy, M. M. (2005, Feb 1). *Gender Differences in Incidence and Age at Onset of Mania and Bipolar Disorder Over a 35-Year Period in Camberwell, England.* Retrieved from The American Journal of Psychiatry: http://ajp.psychiatryonline.org/doi/abs/10.1176/appi.ajp.162.2.257

Paula V. Nunes, O. V. (2007, March). *Lithium and risk for Alzheimer's disease in elderly patients with bipolar disorder.* Retrieved from The British Journal of Psychiatry: http://bjp.rcpsych.org/content/190/4/359.short

Pedersen, T. (n.d.). *Study Probes Distinctions Between Bipolar, Borderline Personality Disorder.* Retrieved from psychcentral.com: https://psychcentral.com/news/2013/10/15/study-probes-distinctions-between-bipolar-borderline-personality-disorder/60743.html

Prof Bruno Müller-Oerlinghausen, M. A. (2002, January 19). *Bipolar.* Retrieved from Science Direct: http://www.sciencedirect.com/science/article/pii/S0140673602074500

Rea, M. M., Tompson, M. C., Miklowitz, D. J., Goldstein, M. J., Hwang, S., & Mintz, J. (2003, June). *Family-focused treatment versus individual treatment for bipolar disorder: Results of a randomized clinical trial.* Retrieved

from Apa Psychnet:
http://psycnet.apa.org/journals/ccp/71/3/482/

Roberts, C. (n.d.). *10 Warning Signs of Bipolar Disorder: Depression and Mania Symptoms*. Retrieved from activebeat.co: http://www.activebeat.co/health-news/10-symptoms-of-bipolar-disorder-are-you-bipolar/?utm_medium=cpc&utm_source=bing&utm_campaign=AB_BNG_US_DESK&utm_content=search&utm_term=symptoms%20of%20bipolar%20mania

S Nassir Ghaemi, M. J. (2002, March 1). *"Cade's Disease" and Beyond: Misdiagnosis, Antidepressant Use, and a Proposed Definition for Bipolar Spectrum Disorder*. Retrieved from The Canadian Journal of Medicine: http://journals.sagepub.com/doi/abs/10.1177/070674370204700202

Samhsa. (n.d.). *Find Help*. Retrieved from http://www.samhsa.gov: http://www.samhsa.gov/treatment/

Steinmann, J. (2015, Dec 22). *How to Deal With Unsupportive Family and Friends*. Retrieved from Huffingtonpost.com: http://www.huffingtonpost.com/jeff-steinmann/how-do-deal-with-unsuppor_b_8856004.html

Swapnil Agrawal, A. A. (2016, December). *FIRST-EPISODE MANIA IN A 9-YEAR-OLD CHILD - A CASE REPORT*. Retrieved from JOURNAL OF RESEARCH IN PSYCHIATRY AND BEHAVIOURAL SCIENCES: http://www.jrpbs.com/latest-articles.php?at_id=19

Tracey, M. N. (2013, July 31). *Bipolar Disorder and Comorbid Borderline Personality Disorder*. Retrieved from Healthyplace.com: http://www.healthyplace.com/blogs/breakingbipolar/2

013/07/bipolar-disorder-comorbid-borderline-personality/

Tracey, N. (2008, December 25). *Dealing with Bipolar Disorder in the Family*. Retrieved from HealthyPlace.com: http://www.healthyplace.com/bipolar-disorder/bipolar-support/dealing-with-bipolar-disorder-in-the-family/

Unknown. (n.d.). *Famous Bipolar People.* Retrieved from famousbipolarpeople.com: http://www.famousbipolarpeople.com/

Wanda K Mohr, P. R. (2001, March). *Bipolar Disorder in CHILDREN*. Retrieved from Healio: http://www.healio.com/psychiatry/journals/jpn/2001-3-39-3/%7B15f1b373-7786-4f7e-ab1e-a3a86428a435%7D/bipolar-disorder-in-children

WebMd. (n.d.). *Children and Teens With Bipolar Disorder.* Retrieved from http://www.webmd.com: http://www.webmd.com/bipolar-disorder/guide/bipolar-children-teens

What Are Hypomania and Mania in Bipolar Disorder? (n.d.). Retrieved from webmd.com: http://www.webmd.com/bipolar-disorder/guide/hypomania-mania-symptoms

www.ingramcontent.com/pod-product-compliance
Lightning Source LLC
Chambersburg PA
CBHW060506290526
45791CB00001B/286